Dog Breed Guide

For Beginners

A Concise Analysis of 50

Dog Breeds (Including Size, Temperament,

Ease of Training, Exercise Needs

And Much More!)

By

Helena Troy

www.MillenniumPublishingLimited.com

Disclaimer

This publication is designed to provide competent and reliable information regarding the subject matter covered. However, it is sold with the understanding that the author is not engaged in rendering medical or other professional advice. Laws and practices often vary from state to state and country to country and if medical or other expert assistance is required, the services of a professional should be sought. The author specifically disclaims any liability that is incurred from the use or application of the contents of this book.

Table of Contents

Introduction

Choosing the perfect dog can be confusing, especially for first-time owners. It's easy to fall in love with a breed and rush into buying a gorgeous Border Collie or an intimidating Doberman Pinscher, but this is a mistake! Buying a dog should be a long, careful process – a new dog is, after all, a new family member.

There are a number of things that potential dog owners need to consider before making the leap. Does the dog breed you've fallen in love with fit in with your lifestyle? If you work eight hours a day, can the dog be left on its own in your home, or will it become stressed and destructive? If you have other pets, will the dog get along with them? Is the dog child-friendly, or will it quickly lose patience?

It works both ways; a new dog must fit in with their owner's lifestyle, but new owners also need to have the skills and patience necessary to provide adequate care for their new canine companion. Prospective dog owners should ask themselves, *Do I have the time to give this breed all the exercise it needs? Do I have the energy to keep up with them? Am I willing to buy it a doggie jacket when the weather gets chilly? Do I want a mellow lap dog or an excitable adventuring buddy?*

This book will analyze fifty unique dog breeds in terms of their relative protection ability, trainability, playfulness, exercise needs and adaptability. If you're a prospective dog owner or even just an enthusiast, read on!

Dog Breed 1 - Whippet

General Information

Dog Name: Whippet

Dog breed Group: Hound dogs

Size Category: Medium dog breeds

Height: Ranges from one foot, six inches to one foot, ten inches (measured from the shoulder).

Weight: Ranges from 18 to 48 pounds.

Lifespan: Ranges from 12 to 15 years.

Brief History

Named for their ability to "move briskly", the Whippet holds the honor of being the fastest accelerating dog in the world. Whilst many types of hound dogs have been used for tracking and scenting prey, none can compete with the Whippet's speed and capture of small prey (e.g. hares) in open fields. The Whippet's origins can be traced back to 17th century England, where they were used by the upper classes for hunting purposes, and appeared in numerous paintings from the time period. In later centuries the Whippet became popular amongst the working class as an alternative to the expensive and sought after greyhound, with whom they share many characteristics.

Dog Breed Characteristics

A. Protection Ability

Given their affectionate and trusting nature, Whippets do not perform well as guard dogs. They are very friendly towards strangers and rarely bark, making them an especially unimposing animal.

Score: 2/10

B. Ease of Training

Whippets are highly intelligent, and they are therefore very receptive to dog training (particularly crate training, due to their preference for a clean sleeping area). Their eagerness to please their owners results in excellent obedience levels. It is important to remember, however, that Whippets' high sensitivity means that they may respond best to clicker training.

Score: 8/10

C. Playfulness

Whippets are full of energy and affection, and so they love to play! A Whippet would be a great choice for a household with children, as they are at their happiest running and playing during the day, and snuggling up to their owners in the evenings. Playfulness in Whippets can be encouraged through early socialization, e.g. taking them on regular walks, and inviting over visitors.

Score: 9/10

D. Exercise needs

Their history of hunting means that Whippets love to run. They need to be walked on a daily basis, for five minutes for every month of their age (e.g. a six month old puppy should have a daily walk lasting 30 minutes). It is important that they are not exercised too heavily, as this will put a strain on their joints.

Score: 7/10

E. Adaptability

Whippets do well in households with children and other dogs, but their hunting instinct can sometimes lead them to injure smaller pets. They are prone to separation anxiety, and also have some difficulty in adapting to temperature changes, especially cold weather.

Score: 5/10

Dog Breed 2 - Yorkshire Terrier

General Information

Dog Name: Yorkshire Terrier (Nickname: Yorkie)

Dog breed Group: Companion dogs

Size Category: Small dog breeds

Height: Ranges from eight to nine inches tall (measured from the shoulder).

Weight: Ranges from 4 to 6 pounds.

Lifespan: Ranges from 12 to 15 years.

Brief History

In addition to being one of the smallest dog breeds in the world, the Yorkshire Terrier is also exceptionally hyperactive and curious. These qualities made the tiny dogs perfect for their original purpose; hunting rats, foxes and badgers in mills and underground burrows. The Yorkshire Terrier was initially brought to England from Scotland in 1861, at which time it was called the Broken-Haired Scotch Terrier. Nine years later the name was changed, in order to pay homage to the county in which the breed had undergone the most development. Modern day Yorkshire Terriers (or "Yorkies") enjoy comfortable lives as beloved household pets, and are considered by many as fashion accessories.

Dog Breed Characteristics

A. Protection Ability

Yorkshire Terriers seem unaware of their lilliputian stature, and will often pick fights with bigger dogs. Far from being able to protect their owners, Yorkies often require their owners to protect them from the fights they have instigated. Socialization from an early age can help to reduce their impulse to fight.

Score: 1/10

B. Ease of Training

It can be difficult to predict how each Yorkshire Terrier will respond to dog training, but the key to a successful training regimen is to begin early. As with all terriers Yorkies can be stubborn, but lots of treats and positivity during short training sessions can help to counteract this. Generally speaking, Yorkies respond well to obedience training but struggle a little with housebreaking.

Score: 6/10

C. Playfulness

With an athletic build and heaps of energy, the Yorkie loves to play! Whilst personality can differ across the breed – some can be cuddly, others can be more rambunctious – no Yorkie likes to be alone. Owners will notice that these tiny dogs will follow them from room to room and are always ready to play. Coupled with their small stature, this quality means that Yorkies are often seen as perpetual puppies.

Score: 8/10

D. Exercise needs

Given their original purpose of hunting and chasing small animals, Yorkshire Terriers are predisposed towards a full workday. They have energy in spades, and so they require lots of physical and mental stimulation. This can take the form of daily walks outside, or even indoor games.

Score: 7/10

E. Adaptability

Yorkies adapt well to new living situations, and the breed is recommended for first-time dog owners. They adapt less easily to changes in weather, and they do not respond well to being left alone. Yorkshire terriers are very sensitive dogs, which means they may become nervous around small children or in noisy environments.

Score: 5/10

Dog Breed 3 - Vizsla

General Information

Dog Name: Vizsla

Dog breed Group: Sporting dogs

Size Category: Medium dog breeds

Height: Ranges from one foot, nine inches to two feet (measured from the shoulder).

Weight: Ranges from 45 to 55 pounds.

Lifespan: Ranges from 12 to 15 years.

Brief History

The Vizsla is a true all-rounder. This breed has existed since the 10th century, but only rose in prominence in 19th century Hungary, when the industrial revolution caused the average huntsman to become more frugal and reduce the number of dogs they owned. There was a need for a single breed which could seek out every type of prey, retrieve from land or water, and also serve as a faithful companion. Only one breed could possibly fill this tall order: the Vizsla. Nowadays the Vizsla is both an excellent hunting dog and a beloved family pet.

Dog Breed Characteristics

A. Protection Ability

The Vizsla is not known for its abilities as a guard dog. They are exuberant by nature, and love meeting new people. Whilst they may bark to warn their owners of intruders, they generally will not have the instinct to attack.

Score: 3/10

B. Ease of Training

As their history would suggest, the Vizsla is both highly intelligent and eager to please. They have been known to outwit both children and adults, and they require lots of interaction and dog training to keep them from becoming bored or destructive. They thrive under structured training, and will always do their best to please their owner.

Score: 9/10

C. Playfulness

Vizslas are extremely affectionate and friendly dogs. They love to be active, whether this means playing with their energetic owners or performing duties as guide dogs, drug detection dogs, search and rescue dogs, etc. Due to their energy and the strong attachments they form to their owners, Vizslas cannot be left for long periods of time without stimulation.

Score: 8/10

D. Exercise needs

As a sporting dog, the Vizsla requires at least one hour of exercise each day (e.g. jogging, swimming, playing “fetch”). With daily exercise, the Vizsla is more likely to be calm around the home, and will have less destructive tendencies.

Score: 8/10

E. Adaptability

Owning a Vizsla can be a challenge. Owners need to be enthusiastic and involved in their dog's care, they can be a handful. They are very sensitive, and cannot abide being left alone for long periods of time. They do not adapt well to cold weather, and so it is recommended that they are kept indoors. This breed may be best suited to an experienced owner.

Score: 3/10

Dog Breed 4 - Weimaraner

General Information

Dog Name: Weimaraner (Nickname: Weim)

Dog breed Group: Sporting dogs

Size Category: Large dog breeds

Height: Ranges from one foot, eleven inches to two feet, three inches (measured from the shoulder).

Weight: Ranges from 55 to 85 pounds.

Lifespan: Ranges from 11 to 13 years.

Brief History

The Weimaraner is a visually stunning animal. Its grey fur and ability to mimic human facial expressions led first century German nobles to limit the availability of the breed by forming the German Weimaraner Club. A descendant of the Bloodhound, the Weimaraner was originally a hunting dog in the forests of Germany, where its stamina, intelligence and scenting ability made it a perfect hunter. Today, the Weimaraners are perhaps best known for their prominence in the work of photographer William Wegman, who believes that their facial expressions convey their personalities in a way no other breed can.

Dog Breed Characteristics

A. Protection Ability

The Weimaraner's guarding instinct can vary across countries; whilst German Weimaraners tend to retain this instinct, the British version of the breed has largely lost this. Generally speaking, this breed is moderately suited to protection – it was, after all, bred to guard as well as to hunt.

Score: 7/10

B. Ease of Training

Given the history of the breed, it's perhaps unsurprising that the Weimaraner is very receptive to dog training. It should also be noted, however, that without firm, consistent training this breed will quickly slip into bad behaviour – perhaps as a result of their high energy levels and hunting instinct. House training this breed can be tricky, and crate training is recommended.

Score: 7/10

C. Playfulness

Weimaraners are full of energy and love to play. They need lots of mental and physical stimulation, which may be challenging for first-time pet-owners. Whilst temperament can vary across the breed, Weimaraners are lively regardless of this. To gauge their Weimaraner's temperament, owners are encouraged to meet the dog's parents for some indication of how their pet's personality may develop.

Score: 8/10

D. Exercise needs

Due to their excess of energy, Weimaraners need rigorous daily exercise. Although they prefer to live indoors, a large fenced yard or garden is also desirable, as this allows them the space to tire themselves out until their hearts' content. Without supervision, however, Weimaraners can over-exert themselves to the point of destroying their owner's gardens. The best way to prevent this is by taking them out daily for at least an hour of exercise.

Score: 9/10

E. Adaptability

Weimaraners do not adapt well outside of their comfort zone, and their owners need to be prepared to invest time and attention into this breed. Weimaraners find it difficult to be alone for long periods of time, and they are very sensitive to loud noises and changes in their environment. This breed is recommended only for experienced dog-owners.

Score: 3/10

Dog Breed 5 - Shiba Inu

General Information

Dog Name: Shiba Inu

Dog breed Group: Companion dogs

Size Category: Small dog breeds

Height: Ranges from one foot, one inch to one foot, five inches (measured from the shoulder).

Weight: Ranges from 17 to 23 pounds.

Lifespan: Ranges from 12 to 16 years.

Brief History

The Shiba Inu is the smallest of the six distinct breeds of dog that are native to Japan. It can be seen in ancient drawings dating back to the third century, in which it is depicted chasing small animals. This breed is known for being quick and nimble, qualities that made them perfect hunting dogs during Japan's period of military rule (Kamakura Shogunate). Nowadays, these small dogs are most often found in Japan and the USA, where they are popular companion dogs.

Dog Breed Characteristics

A. Protection Ability

Their natural distrust of strangers makes the Shiba Inu a passable watch dog. Whilst they will bark to alert their owners of unfamiliar people, they generally will not attack or even approach strangers.

Score: 4/10

B. Ease of Training

Despite their intelligence, the Shiba Inu is notoriously difficult to train. They are tremendously independent, and so whilst they may understand what their owner is asking of them, they will not always want to comply. The best approach to training the Shiba Inu is make them believe the obedience is their idea. Fortunately, this breed is naturally clean and very receptive to housebreaking.

Score: 5/10

C. Playfulness

The Shiba Inu is a moderately energetic breed which forms tight attachments to their owners and children. This means that whilst they are generally very playful with people they know, they can be a little aloof with strangers. This breed has described as “cat-like” in its behaviours; it enjoys being lavished in attention, but it's also perfectly content with lounging around the house alone.

Score: 6/10

D. Exercise needs

Whilst it's true that Shiba Inus are not the most energetic of breeds, they do need daily exercise in order to stave off boredom and aggression. They typically are happiest with one daily walk, during which they must stay on the lease, due to their prey instinct and their potential for dog-aggression.

Score: 5/10

E. Adaptability

The Shiba Inu is very adaptable to changes in their environment, and they are suited to apartment living. They can be left alone during the day, and they behave well around children (provided that they are treated respectfully).

Score: 8/10

Dog Breed 1-5 Quiz

We have created this fun quiz to help you consolidate what you learn in this book. While we appreciate any given question may have more than one correct answer, we implore you to select the best option (out of the 4 options presented) based on the *information in this book*.

The solution to this quiz can be found in *Appendix A* at the end of this book.

1. Due to their affectionate and trusting nature, one of the below dog breed is likely not to perform well as a guard dog. Which is it?
   a) Weimaraner
   b) Whippet
   c) Shiba Inu
   d) Yorkshire Terrier

2. Renowned for their ability to *move briskly*, which dog breed holds the honor of being the fastest accelerating dog in the world?
   a) Vizsla
   b) Whippet
   c) Shiba Inu
   d) Yorkshire Terrier

3. One of the below dog breeds will make a great choice for a household with children as they are at their happiest running and playing. Which is it?
   a) Vizsla
   b) Whippet
   c) Shiba Inu
   d) Yorkshire Terrier

4. This dog breed was renowned for hunting rats, foxes and badgers in mills and underground burrows.
   a) Vizsla

b) Whippet
c) Shiba Inu
d) Yorkshire Terrier

5. An all-rounder, this dog can seek out every type of prey, retrieve from land or water, and also serve as a faithful companion.
   a) Vizsla
   b) Weimaraner
   c) Shiba Inu
   d) Yorkshire Terrier

6. A descendant of the bloodhound, this dog was well known for its ability to mimic human facial expressions.
   a) Vizsla
   b) Weimaraner
   c) Shiba Inu
   d) Yorkshire Terrier

7. Quick and nimble, this dog made for the perfect hunting dog during Japan's period of military rule
   a) Vizsla
   b) Weimaraner
   c) Shiba Inu
   d) Yorkshire Terrier

8. Despite its intelligence, this dog is notoriously difficult to train. They are tremendously independent, and so whilst they may understand what their owner is asking of them, they will not always want to comply.
   a) Weimaraner

b) Shiba Inu

c) Whippet

d) Yorkshire Terrier

9. Very adaptable to changes in their environment, this dog breed is perfectly suited to apartment living.

   a) Whippet

   b) Yorkshire Terrier

   c) Vizsla

   d) Shiba Inu

Dog Breed 6 - Shih Tzu

General Information

Dog Name: Shih Tzu

Dog breed Group: Companion dogs

Size Category: Small dog breeds

Height: Ranges from nine inches to ten inches (measured from the shoulder).

Weight: Ranges from 9 to 16 pounds.

Lifespan: Ranges from 10 to 16 years.

Brief History

Few breeds can rival the regal history of the Shih Tzu: bred for no reason beyond providing companionship to Chinese royals, these dogs were bred during the Ming and Machu dynasties, and were rarely seen outside the palaces of the royal court. A popular myth suggests that Buddha travelled with a Shih Tzu which protected him from enemies by transforming into a lion (the name itself translates to little lion). In the twentieth century Shih Tzus were often given as gifts to European noblemen, and eventually arrived in the USA soon afterwards.

Dog Breed Characteristics

A. Protection Ability

The Shih Tzu was bred as a companion dog, and so it isn't suited to guarding or protecting its owner. They do, however, have excellent hearing. This makes them good watchdogs, and they will alert their owner when they hear something out of the ordinary.

Score: 3/10

B. Ease of Training

Intelligence does not always guarantee an easy dog training process, and the Shih Tzu is a prime example of this. This breed will only comply with its owners orders if they feel there's something to be gained, and they are typically unexcited by treats or toys. They do, however, crave approval from their owners, and so the best way to train a Shih Tzu is to develop a strong bond with them. Their short attention span also means that short training sessions may be the most effective approach.

Score: 4/10

C. Playfulness

Whilst Shih Tzus are very playful, they do not have as much energy as other breeds. They are most commonly found snuggling in their owners laps, relishing being the centre of attention, rather than racing around the house.

Score: 5/10

D. Exercise needs

As a brachycephalic breed, Shih Tzus can get easily winded and sometimes struggle with long walks. They need to exercise every day, but this can usually be achieved through them following their owners around the house. They do not have a predator instinct, and so they often get bored when playing "fetch".

Score: 2/10

E. Adaptability

This breed is happy living in both sprawling estates and city apartments. By nature they are relatively adaptable; they cope well with being left alone, and can play well with children (provided there is no rough play). Shih Tzus can get uncomfortable in hot weather due to their short faces, but this can be remedied by keeping them in an air-conditioned room on hot days.

Score: 8/10

Dog Breed 7 - Siberian Husky

General Information

Dog Name: Siberian Husky

Dog breed Group: Working dogs

Size Category: Medium dog breeds

Height: Ranges from one foot, eight inches to one foot, eleven inches (measured from the shoulder).

Weight: Ranges from 35 to 60 pounds.

Lifespan: Ranges from 12 to 15 years.

Brief History

The arresting beauty of the Siberian Husky can be attributed to its ancient and pure lineage. The breed was developed by the Chukchi hunting people, who needed strong sled dogs to help them transport loads through the Siberian Arctic. The Chukchi were deeply religious, and believed the gates of heaven to be guarded by two Siberian Huskies. In the early twentieth century Siberian Huskies were used as sled dogs in Alaska during the gold rush, and not long after the breed sadly disappeared from their native Siberia completely.

Dog Breed Characteristics

A. Protection Ability

Generally speaking, Siberian Huskies are not suitable guard dogs or watch dogs. They are very trusting of strangers, and they're happy to approach and play with anybody.

Score: 1/10

B. Ease of Training

Due to their identity as a pack dog, Siberian Huskies need to know that their owner is the leader of the pack; once this is established, training should progress smoothly. This breed will occasionally test their owner and attempt to take leadership themselves, but owners can easily combat this by re-establishing their authority. By making Siberian Huskies wait to eat, owners can clearly demonstrate that they are the keeper of the food, and therefore the leader of the pack. Training a Siberian Husky is difficult, and should be attempted only by an experienced pet-owner.

Score: 4/10

C. Playfulness

Siberian Huskies have lots of energy and are generally very affectionate. They are friendly towards their owners, children and strangers, many of whom often find it difficult to keep up with the playful animal.

Score: 7/10

D. Exercise needs

Siberian Huskies require up to an hour of rigorous exercise every day, and enjoy accompanying their owners on hikes or outdoor sports. This breed is especially energetic, and Siberian Huskies often get lost when they become overly focused on chasing small prey, or simply feel an urge to run.

Score: 9/10

E. Adaptability

Owners beware: Siberian Huskies demand a lot of attention. They aren't well suited to apartment living, and they cannot tolerate being left alone while their owner is at work. They are quite sensitive, meaning that they become nervous and jumpy in loud environments. Many novice owners adopt Siberian Huskies after falling in love with the breed's distinctive beauty, and are quickly shocked by the level of care they require.

Score: 4/10

Dog Breed 8 - Shetland Sheepdog

General Information

Dog Name: Shetland Sheepdog (Nickname: Sheltie)

Dog breed Group: Herding dogs

Size Category: Medium dog breeds

Height: Ranges from one foot, one inch to one foot, four inches (measured from the shoulder).

Weight: Upwards of 20 pounds.

Lifespan: Ranges from 12 to 15 years.

Brief History

This herding dog gets its name from the Shetland Islands of Scotland, where the breed first emerged in the eighteenth century. A cross between several breeds including the Scandinavian Spitz, the Border Collie and the Pomeranian, the Shetland Sheepdog's original purpose was to shoo away birds from their owner's sheep. Over time, farmers realised that they could capitalise on their Shelties' diminutive stature by breeding them to be even smaller and fluffier, and selling them to tourists. This high amount of cross-breeding led to many arguments about how the original Shetland Sheepdog should look. It was eventually decided by the English and

Scottish Kennel Clubs that it should resemble a Rough Collie in miniature.

Dog Breed Characteristics

A. Protection Ability

Shelties were bred to herd sheep, and as such they are very vocal. They are typically on alert and will bark loudly when faced with any potential danger, be it the postman, an airplane, or even the sound of a hair dryer. Their instinct is to warn and defend their owners from harm, but they will not attack aggressors.

Score: 7/10

B. Ease of Training

Their working background means that Shetland Sheepdogs have an innate desire to perform tasks and an abundance of energy. Their intelligence and sensitive nature means that they can react to their owners tone of voice, and are therefore quite easy to train. They excel in obedience competitions, especially in events such as flyball, tracking and herding.

Score: 9/10

C. Playfulness

As a pack animal, Shetland Sheepdogs are endlessly loyal and attentive to their owners, or their "pack". They are known to be very intuitive; they will be hyperactive and playful when their owner is happy, and quietly affectionate when their owner is sad. They love to be with people, and will follow their owners from room to room.

Score: 7/10

D. Exercise needs

Shelties are predisposexd to long working days, and so they need lots of exercise to burn off excess energy. They enjoy long runs and playing fetch, and will safely play for hours on end with children.

Score: 9/10

E. Adaptability

This breed is generally not very adaptable. Whilst they are small enough to live in apartments, they are much happier with space to roam throughout the day. They dislike being left alone for long periods of time, and they are highly sensitive to their environment. Caring for a Shetland Sheepdog requires a patient owner who is willing to invest time into their pet's training.

Score: 4/10

Dog Breed 9 - French Bulldog

General Information

Dog Name: French Bulldog (Nickname: Frenchie)

Dog breed Group: Companion dogs

Size Category: Small dog breeds

Height: Ranges from eleven inches to one foot (measured from the shoulder).

Weight: Ranges from 16 to 28 pounds

Lifespan: Ranges from 11 to 14 years

Brief History

The French Bulldog is the result of a collaboration between England, France and the USA. English Bulldogs were very popular in nineteenth century England, and when lace-makers emigrated to Northern France during the Industrial Revolution many took the little dogs with them. The breed was loved by the French, and their copious cross-breeding resulted in the distinctive French Bulldog (or Bouledogue Francais). It wasn't long before the Americans visiting France took an interest. They brought the French Bulldog to the USA, and decided to breed the dog with the upright bat ears for which the breed is now famous.

Dog Breed Characteristics

A. Protection Ability

Frenchies are not known for their ability to protect. They make excellent companions and are friendly to almost everybody they meet, but this unfortunately this trusting nature means that they are not good guard dogs or watch dogs.

Score: 2/10

B. Ease of Training

This breed is intelligent, stubborn and has a short attention span. This can make dog training a challenge, and owners will need to use short training sessions with lots of treats and fun in order to keep their French Bulldog's interest.

Score: 5/10

C. Playfulness

Truly a companion dog, the Frenchie craves attention and will often play the clown to amuse its owner. This breed is a fantastic pet for the elderly, as it is endlessly playful but does not so much energy that it becomes unmanageable.

Score: 6/10

D. Exercise needs

French Bulldogs require just fifteen minutes of exercise each day. They can get this exercise either in the form of walks or simply by playing with their owners. It can be dangerous to exercise them in the hotter months, as they are susceptible to heatstroke.

Score: 2/10

E. Adaptability

Provided that they are kept inside and given enough attention, Frenchies are easily satisfied. They are suitable for apartment living and are not overly sensitive to loud noises or changes in their environment. They don't do well in extremely hot or cold climates, but this can be dealt with by ensuring they have adequate shelter.

Score: 7/10

Dog Breed 10 - German Shepherd

General Information

Dog Name: German Shepherd

Dog breed Group: Herding dogs

Size Category: Large dog breeds

Height: Ranges from one foot, ten inches to two feet, two inches (measured form the shoulder)

Weight: Ranges from 75 to 95 pounds.

Lifespan: Ranges from 10 to 14 years.

Brief History

In nineteenth century Germany, herding dogs were commonly used to drive and protect farmers' herds. Whilst these dogs were undoubtedly skilled, they had never been developed into a distinct breed. Max von Stephanitz, an ex-cavalry captain, believed that he could develop one superior German herding dog which encapsulated all of the traits seen in herding dogs (such as intelligence and athleticism). The German Shepherd was eventually born, and the breed went on to work in World War I as messengers, rescuers, and Red Cross dogs. One such dog was taken home after the war by an American soldier, and went on to star in 26 films as Rin Tin Tin. More recently, German Shepherds attained fame as search and rescue dogs during the

9/11 terrorist attacks.

Dog Breed Characteristics

A. Protection Ability

German Shepherds are strong, loyal and very protective, qualities which make them excellent watchdogs. It takes this breed a little longer than others to form bonds, but once they feel attached to their owners they will do everything in their power to protect them.

Score: 8/10

B. Ease of Training

This breed is intelligent and sensitive, and can thus be trained to do almost anything; from fetching a newspaper to seeking out an avalanche victim. They do well with obedience training, and crate training can help to lessen their separation anxiety.

Score: 9/10

C. Playfulness

German Shepherds are energetic, intense and exceedingly playful. They are great with children, and will often play for hours. When deprived of adequate play, these dogs will often become restless and may chew furniture or bark excessively.

Score: 8/10

D. Exercise needs

As they were bred to herd flocks on a daily basis, German Shepherds require rigorous exercise every day. They need both physical and mental stimulation, which can be achieved through daily runs or obedience programs. Without regular exercise, German Shepherds will show their agitation by chewing, digging and barking.

Score: 9/10

E. Adaptability

This breed is highly sensitive, and so it takes a practiced owner to know how best to care for a German Shepherd. They need a great deal of living space, and they do not tolerate being alone very well.

Score: 4/10

Dog Breed 6-10 Quiz

The solution to this quiz can be found in *Appendix B* at the end of this book.

1. This dog breed was particularly bred as a companion dog so isn't suited to protecting its owner. Their short attention span means that short training sessions may be the most effective approach to dog training.
   a) German Shepherd
   b) Shih Tzu
   c) French Bulldog
   d) Siberian husky

2. Due to their identity as a pack dog, this dog breed need to know that their owner is the leader of the pack; once this is established, training should progress smoothly.
   a) German Shepherd
   b) Shih Tzu
   c) French Bulldog
   d) Siberian husky

3. The Chukchi hunting people, who needed strong sled dogs to help them transport loads through the Arctic, developed this breed. Can you identify the dog breed?
   a) German Shepherd
   b) Shih Tzu
   c) French Bulldog
   d) Siberian husky

4. This breed will only comply with its owners orders if they feel there's something to be gained, and they are typically unexcited by treats or toys. They do, however, crave approval from their owners, and so the best way to train them is to develop a strong bond with them
   a) German Shepherd

b) Shih Tzu
c) Shetland Sheepdog
d) Siberian husky

5. A cross between several breeds including the Scandinavian Spitz, the Border Collie and the Pomeranian, this dog breed's original purpose was to shoo away birds from their owner's farm.
   a) German Shepherd
   b) Shih Tzu
   c) Shetland Sheepdog
   d) Siberian husky

6. Their working background means that this dog breed has an innate desire to perform tasks and an abundance of energy. Their intelligence and sensitive nature means that they can react to their owners tone of voice, and are therefore quite easy to train
   a) Siberian Husky
   b) German Shepherd
   c) Shetland Sheepdog
   d) French Bulldog

7. Truly a companion dog, this dog breed craves attention and will often play the clown to amuse its owner. It will make a fantastic pet for the elderly.
   a) Siberian Husky
   b) German Shepherd
   c) Shetland Sheepdog
   d) French Bulldog

8. This dog breed worked in World War 1 as a messenger, rescuer, and Red Cross dog.
   a) Siberian Husky

b) German Shepherd

c) Shetland Sheepdog

d) French Bulldog

9. As they were bred to herd flocks on a daily basis, this dog breed requires rigorous exercise every day. They need both physical and mental stimulation, which can be achieved through daily runs or obedience programs.

   a) Siberian Husky

   b) Shih Tzu

   c) Shetland Sheepdog

   d) German Shepherd

10. This dog breed isn't well suited to apartment living, and cannot tolerate being left alone while their owner is at work. They are quite sensitive, meaning that they become nervous and jumpy in loud environments.

    a) Siberian Husky

    b) Shih Tzu

    c) Shetland Sheepdog

    d) German Shepherd

Dog Breed 11 - Golden Retriever

General Information

Dog Name: Golden Retriever

Dog breed Group: Sporting dogs

Size Category: Large dog breeds

Height: Ranges from one foot, nine inches to two feet (measured form the shoulder).

Weight: Ranges from 55 to 75 pounds.

Lifespan: Ranges from 10 to 12 years.

Brief History

The Golden Retriever came into existence in the late nineteenth century when Lord Tweedmouth, a Scottish nobleman, decided to develop a breed which could scent, retrieve and be a loyal companion. Lord Tweedmouth originally bred a yellow coloured Flat Coated Retriever to a Water Spaniel, and through several rounds of cross-breeding he eventually bred the dog of which he had dreamt: the Golden Retriever.

Dog Breed Characteristics

A. Protection Ability

Whilst their friendliness makes them poor guard dogs, Golden Retrievers are good watchdogs. They will readily alert their owners of any suspicious occurrences, but they are ultimately very trusting of strangers and do not have the instinct to attack.

Score: 5/10

B. Ease of Training

Golden Retrievers respond very well to dog training. They are eager to please, and for this reason they are the top choice for service and therapy dogs. They do not respond well to discipline, but with gentle training and lots of rewards, this breed is typically very easy to train.

Score: 9/10

C. Playfulness

Golden Retrievers are generally very playful and have a sunny temperament. It should be noted, however, that the huge demand for this breed has led to a high number of disreputable breeders whose focus is making money, rather than breeding happy dogs. Prospective owners should check they are purchasing from a reputable source to avoid puppies with unstable temperaments.

Score: 8/10

D. Exercise needs

This breed has lots of energy, and should be walked every day. Their playful nature means that they'll also be happy with getting their daily exercise through games and outdoor activities. They are generally evenly tempered, and so do not require hours of exercise.

Score: 6/10

E. Adaptability

Golden Retrievers are highly sensitive, and need lots of living space. Whilst novice owners can adequately care for this breed, they should be prepared for their constant need to be around people, and their boisterous nature.

Score: 6/10

Dog Breed 12 - Doberman Pinscher

General Information

Dog Name: Doberman Pinscher (Nicknames: Dobie, Doberman)

Dog breed Group: Working dogs

Size Category: Large dog breeds

Height: Ranges from two feet to two feet, four inches (measured from the shoulder).

Weight: Ranges from 60 to 80 pounds.

Lifespan: Ranges from 10 to 13 years.

Brief History

The Doberman Pinscher is a protector. In nineteenth century Germany, a tax collector called Louis Dobermann would often bring a dog to accompany him to houses in dangerous areas. When he decided to breed a dog who could be both a faithful companion and strong companion, the Dobermann Pinscher was born. It is thought that this breed was developed by cross-breeding the Rottweiler, German Pinscher and Black and Tan Terrier, amongst others. The Doberman Pinscher was soon regarded to be a “super dog”, and was brought to the USA. Nowadays, the coarser aspects of the Doberman Pinscher's personality has been bred out, and it is a popular family pet.

Dog Breed Characteristics

A. Protection Ability

Doberman Pinschers were bred to be personal protectors, and so this is what they do best. They are muscular, intimidating, and they will not hesitate to attack when commanded.

Score: 9/10

B. Ease of Training

As one of the smartest dog breeds, Dobies are quite easy to train. Their ability to learn quickly means that they can also get bored quickly, and so it is important that owners keep training sessions fresh and interesting, with lots of praise.

Score: 9/10

C. Playfulness

Temperament can differ drastically across the breed. As with all dog breeds, socialisation from an early age is key to ensuring a playful pet. Doberman Pinschers have the potential and the energy to be very playful, and is generally very keen to be part of a loving family.

Score: 6/10

D. Exercise needs

Dobies are full of energy that needs to burned off throughout the day. They should be walked briskly at least twice a day, and the ideal home for this breed will have a large, fenced back garden where they can run freely.

Score: 8/10

E. Adaptability

Doberman Pinschers require a lot of love and attention, and may not be suitable for first-time owners. They are sensitive to their surroundings, and are especially intolerant of cold weather.

Score: 5/10

Dog Breed 13 - Collie

General Information

Dog Name: Collie

Dog breed Group: Herding dogs

Size Category: Medium dog breeds

Height: Ranges from one foot, ten inches to two feet, two inches (measured from the shoulder).

Weight: Ranges from 50 to 70 pounds.

Lifespan: Ranges from 10 to 14 years.

Brief History

The Collie originally hails from the Scottish Highlands, where it was used to herd cattle, sheep, goats and pigs. Collies were not particularly common until 1860, when Queen Victoria fell in love with the breed's beautiful appearance and placid temperament during a visit to her

Scottish estate. She brought some of them back to England, where they quickly rose in popularity. Although originally working dogs, Collies were soon being bred for their good looks and performance in dog shows. They also became immensely popular across the pond, with one American Collie appearing on television as the popular character "Lassie" for a number of years.

Dog Breed Characteristics

A. Protection Ability

Collies are first and foremost herding dogs, and it is difficult to train them to be guard dogs. In the Scottish Highlands they were typically loaned between farmers, and so they are naturally trusting of strangers. Whilst they do have an impressive bark, this is as far as their protective abilities go.

Score: 4/10

B. Ease of Training

This breed is particularly receptive to dog training. Their intelligence and sensitivity means that they learn quickly, but they also grow bored with repetitive training programs, such as obedience training. They must be given an incentive to obey, and they respond best to novel, short training sessions.

Score: 7/10

C. Playfulness

Collies are exuberant family dogs, and they enjoy being involved in all aspects of family life. They can be trusted to play gently with children as well as protect them from harm. Whilst temperaments can differ between dogs, generally speaking Collies are very sweet-natured and playful.

Score: 7/10

D. Exercise needs

Collies require daily exercise, ideally in the form of a brisk walk. They have moderate energy levels, meaning that they will be happy with simply playing with their owners or running around the garden each day.

Score: 6/10

E. Adaptability

Overall, Collies adapt rather well to their surroundings, although they do really need a large living space. They can tolerate most weathers (due to their origins in the windy Scottish Highlands), and are suitable for novice owners.

Score: 7/10

Dog Breed 14 - Chihuahua

General Information

Dog Name: Chihuahua

Dog breed Group: Companion dogs

Size Category: Small dog breeds

Height: Ranges from six inches to nine inches (measured from the shoulder).

Weight: Ranges from three to six pounds.

Lifespan: Ranges from 10 to 18 years.

Brief History

The exact origins of the Chihuahua are somewhat of a mystery. Some people believe it to be a descendant of the Techichi, a small dog from the Toltec civilization in ninth century South America. It was thought that the Techichi could see into the future, and would guide deceased souls to the underworld. Others believe the Chihuahua is the result of cross-breeding between hairless dogs from China and small dogs from Spain. In 1850 the Chihuahua was first discovered in the Mexican state of Chihuahua, from which it takes its name, and it went on to become popular decades later in the 1960s.

Dog Breed Characteristics

A. Protection Ability

Whilst the Chihuahua thinks itself large and intimidating, in truth it's no match for other breeds. It will often start fights with much larger dogs, and puts itself in danger of harm. For this reason, owners must be vigilant in ensuring their pet is always safe. The Chihuahua is, however, very wary of strangers, and this quality makes it a good watchdog.

Score: 4/10

B. Ease of Training

Chihuahuas are relatively easy to train and they excel in sports and obedience tasks. They are also easy to housebreak, given a consistent schedule is established. Chihuahuas respond best to positive reinforcement and treats – as long as these elements are present, any training program should progress smoothly.

Score: 8/10

C. Playfulness

Chihuahuas are very playful, and are known for their bold personalities. Chihuahuas often form close bonds to single individuals, which can make them demanding, but this can be prevented with training. They are also endlessly curious, and so they often escape their homes in search of adventure.

Score: 7/10

D. Exercise needs

The Chihuahua does not require nearly as much exercise as other breeds, but they will exhaust themselves if given the chance. They enjoy walks and games, but owners must watch them carefully to ensure they do not tire themselves out, especially on hot summer days.

Score: 2/10

E. Adaptability

This breed is somewhat adaptable. They are suitable for apartment living, can easily be handled by first-time pet-owners, but they strongly dislike being alone and can even be clingy towards their owners. They are particularly sensitive to changes in the weather; on hot days they may over-exert themselves to the point of exhaustion, and on cold days they must wrap up in a warm jumper or risk shivering.

Score: 5/10

Dog Breed 15- Chow Chow

General Information

Dog Name: Chow Chow

Dog breed Group: Working dogs

Size Category: Medium dog breeds

Height: Ranges from one foot, five inches to one foot, eight inches (measured from the shoulder).

Weight: Ranges from 40 to 70 pounds.

Lifespan: Ranges from 9 to 15 years.

Brief History

The Chow Chow holds the honour of being one of the oldest breeds known to man. Images of the breed can be seen in paintings from the Han dynasty of ancient China, and it is thought that they originated in Mongolian nomadic tribes three thousand years ago. The Chow Chow was a versatile breed that the Mongolians used for guarding cattle, as well as hunting wolves and leopards. When the breed came to China its hardiness made it perfect for working as a sled dog in the winter, and sadly it was frequently slaughtered for its meat and fur. The breed later made it out of Asia, and became very popular in the USA and across Europe.

Dog Breed Characteristics

A. Protection Ability

Chow Chows were bred by the ancient Mongolians to guard and herd cattle, and so protection is in their blood. This breed is regarded as one of the best guard dogs, and is exceptionally strong-willed.

Score: 8/10

B. Ease of Training

Training this breed can be a challenge, as they do not have the instinct to please their owner. Their primary concern is themselves, and they do not respond to positive reinforcement and rewards in the same way as other breeds. With a skilled and determined owner the Chow Chow can indeed be trained, but it will be a slow process.

Score: 4/10

C. Playfulness

Chow Chows are not overly fond of playtime. They will often form strong bonds to one owner, but they are not terribly affectionate and tend to prefer their own company.

Score: 2/10

D. Exercise needs

Whilst all dogs need exercise, the Chow Chow doesn't require much. They will be happy with one short walk each day, as they do not have a huge amount of energy. They can even get their daily exercise by simply walking around the home and garden.

Score: 3/10

E. Adaptability

Chow Chows are happy living in any setting, provided that they have access to shade during hot weather. They are not terribly sensitive but they can lack patience with small children, which must be taken into consideration by prospective owners.

Score: 8/10

Dog Breed 11-15 Quiz

The solution to this quiz can be found in *Appendix C* at the end of this book.

1. When Lord Tweedmouth, a Scottish nobleman, decided to develop a breed which could scent, retrieve and be a loyal companion. He created:
   a) Doberman Pinscher
   b) Golden Retriever
   c) Chihuahua
   d) Collie

2. This dog breed responds very well to dog training and, as such, can make very good service and therapy dogs.
   a) Doberman Pinscher
   b) Golden Retriever
   c) Chihuahua
   d) Collie

3. This dog breed is the ultimate protector. Created in nineteenth century Germany by a tax collector called Louise Dobermann who needed a faithful and strong dog to accompany him to houses in dangerous areas.
   a) Chow chow
   b) Chihuahua
   c) Dobie
   d) Collie

4. Muscular, intimidating, will not hesitate to attack when commanded - this dog breed is the ultimate protector. Created in nineteenth century Germany by a tax collector called Louise Dobermann who needed a faithful and strong dog to accompany him to houses in dangerous areas.
   a) Chow chow

b) Chihuahua

c) Dobie

d) Collie

5. This dog breed was not particularly common until 1860, when Queen Victoria fell in love with it's beautiful appearance and placid temperament during a visit to her Scottish estate.

   a) Chow chow

   b) Golden Retriever

   c) Dobie

   d) Collie

6. An exuberant family dog, this dog breed enjoys being involved in all aspects of family life. It can be trusted to play gently with children as well as protect them from harm.

   a) Golden Retriever

   b) Collie

   c) Chow chow

   d) Doberman Pinscher

7. Believed to have the ability to see into the future and guide deceased souls to the underworld, this dog breed takes its name from a city in Mexico.

   a) Collie

   b) Chihuahua

   c) Golden Retriever

   d) Doberman Pinscher

8. Bold and very playful, this dog breed can often form a close bond to a single individual, which can make it demanding. It is also endlessly curious, and so can escape in search of adventure

a) Golden Retriever
b) Chow chow
c) Chihuahua
d) Doberman Pinscher

9. This dog breed holds the honour of being one of the oldest breeds known to man. Images of the breed can be seen in paintings from the Han dynasty of ancient China and it is thought that they originated in Mongolian nomadic tribes 3000 years ago!
   a) Golden Retriever
   b) Collie
   c) Chow chow
   d) Doberman Pinscher

10. Training this breed can be a challenge, as they do not have the instinct to please their owner. Their primary concern is themselves, and they do not respond well to positive reinforcement and rewards in the same way as other breeds.
    a) Golden Retriever
    b) Doberman Pinscher
    c) Chihuahua
    d) Chow chow

Dog Breed 16 - Chinese Shar-Pei

General Information

Dog Name: Chinese Shar-Pei

Dog breed Group: Working dogs

Size Category: Large dog breeds

Height: Ranges from one foot, six inches to one foot, eight inches (measured from the shoulder).

Weight: Ranges from 40 to 55 pounds.

Lifespan: Ranges from 8 to 12 years.

Brief History

Originally a peasant's dog in ancient China, the Shar-Pei had a multitude of jobs including hunter, guard dog and even dog fighter (presumably because its loose skin was difficult for opponents to grip). Disaster struck for the Shar-Pei when the Chinese communist rulers decided to oppose domestic pet ownership, and thousands of Shar-Peis were slaughtered along with many other Chinese breeds. A few lucky survivors were imported to Hong Kong and later the USA, where the breed once again began to flourish. To date, the Chinese Shar-Pei is one of the rarest breeds in the world, but luckily they are no longer in danger of extinction.

Dog Breed Characteristics

A. Protection Ability

Despite their adorable appearance, the Chinese Shar-Pei has a strong instinct to protect their owners, and they are instantly suspicious of strangers entering the home. They can be aggressive towards intruders, and will do everything they can to protect their "family". They are regarded as one of the top guard dogs.

Score: 9/10

B. Ease of Training

Training a Shar-Pei is easily done, given that dog training starts from a very young age. This breed is very strong-willed and so it will take a determined owner to tame this tough fighter.

Score: 6/10

C. Playfulness

The Shar-Pei is deeply loyal to its owners, but it is not a particularly playful dog. They enjoy being around their owners but are reluctant to play, and they are usually aloof with strangers.

Score: 2/10

D. Exercise needs

Shar-Peis do not need much exercise at all. They can get their daily fill by following their owners from room to room, and they don't have the energy to do much more than this!

Score: 3/10

E. Adaptability

The Shar-Pei can tolerate many changes to its environment. Whilst they like being around their owners they can be left alone during the day, and they are suitable for novice owners. As long as they are kept warm and safe from the elements, the Shar-Pei will be content.

Score: 8/10

Dog Breed 17 - Dachshund

General Information

Dog Name: Dachshund (Nickname: Sausage dog)

Dog breed Group: Hound dogs

Size Category: Small dog breeds

Height: Ranges from eight inches to nine inches (measured from the shoulder).

Weight: Ranges from 16 to 32 pounds.

Lifespan: Ranges from 12 to 15 years.

Brief History

Despite its adorable appearance, the Dachshund is a formidable hunter. These tiny dogs originate from fifteenth century Germany, where their small bodies were perfect for sneaking into badger burrows and fighting them to the death. Their stubby legs made them efficient diggers, and their barks were loud enough to alert their owners when they found their prey underground. In the nineteenth century the Dachshund became a fixture in Queen Victoria's royal court, and more recently the breed has become one of the most popular family dogs in the USA.

Dog Breed Characteristics

A. Protection Ability

The Dachshund is an excellent watchdog. Their loud barks will attract attention to any suspicious activity, and they are fiercely protective of their home and owners. They will bark with very little provocation, which can sometimes be irritating for their owners.

Score: 8/10

B. Ease of Training

Dog training can be a challenge, as Dachshunds have a short attention span and don't always see the point in certain lessons, such as going to the toilet outside rather than in the house. Despite their stubbornness they are very intelligent, and with a dedicated trainer they have the potential to develop into well-behaved pets.

Score: 7/10

C. Playfulness

Personality can vary according to this breed's coat type, as different coats indicate different cross-breeds. Generally speaking, Dachshunds are very playful but their fragile bodies can become easily damaged. It's important that owners watch their pets carefully, as many Dachshunds slip discs in their backs by jumping down from furniture.

Score: 8/10

D. Exercise needs

Dachshunds have lots of energy, and should have a moderate amount of daily exercise. Two 10 minutes walks each day should be sufficient. It's very easy for Dachshunds to over-eat and become lazy, so it is crucial that they are exercised each day.

Score: 5/10

E. Adaptability

The Dachshund adapts well to apartment living, and is comfortable with children. Whilst it is quite sensitive, it can tolerate being left alone throughout the day and is fine with most weather conditions.

Score: 6/10

Dog Breed 18 - Dalmatian

General Information

Dog Name: Dalmatian

Dog breed Group: Companion dogs

Size Category: Large dog breeds

Height: Ranges from one foot, seven inches to two feet (measured from the shoulder).

Weight: Ranges from 48 to 55 pounds.

Lifespan: Ranges from 13 to 16 years.

Brief History

Before rising to fame in the Disney film 101 Dalmatians (1961), this breed roamed across Europe with bands of gypsy nomads. They acted as sentinels on the Dalmatia-Croatia border during wartime, and later became impressive circus performers. Dalmatians are intelligent and boast an excellent memory, and so they've thrived as firehouse dogs, coaching dogs, retrievers, and many other careers.

Dog Breed Characteristics

A. Protection Ability

As former guard dogs, Dalmatians are able to offer their owners a good degree of protection. They are aloof with strangers, and will only bark when they feel their owner is in danger. They are generally not aggressive.

Score: 7/10

B. Ease of Training

Due to their intelligence and headstrong nature, it is important that Dalmatians are trained with a firm hand from an early age (they will not, however, respond to an overly harsh style). Inconsistent training will lead them to believe that they are in charge, but if properly trained Dalmatians will grow up to be obedient and receptive.

Score: 6/10

C. Playfulness

Dalmatians are very aware of their surroundings and love to make their owners laugh. They enjoy energetic playtime and always want to be involved in family activities.

Score: 8/10

D. Exercise needs

Dalmatians have lots of energy, and one of their favorite ways to exercise is to rough-house with their owners or young children. They're a rowdy breed and can often become destructive in the absence of a lively daily exercise routine.

Score: 9/10

E. Adaptability

Whilst Dalmatians can tolerate being left alone for short periods of time, and are not particularly sensitive to changes in their environment, they are still a challenging breed to care for. They need a large living space, ideally with a spacious garden, and are best-suited to experienced dog-owners.

Score: 6/10

Dog Breed 19 - Bullmastiff

General Information

Dog Name: Bullmastiff

Dog breed Group: Working dogs

Size Category: Large dog breeds

Height: Ranges from two feet to two feet, three inches (measured from the shoulder).

Weight: Ranges from 100 to 130 pounds.

Lifespan: Ranges from 8 to 10 years.

Brief History

The Bullmastiff is the only guard dog breed to originate from England, and is (as the name suggests) a cross between a Bulldog and a Mastiff. During the nineteenth century, large English estates were often at risk from poachers, and gamekeepers needed a sturdy dog to help fend them off. The solution was the Bullmastiff; a dog which could quietly track and subdue poachers. Poaching gradually declined, but the Bullmastiff remains today a tenacious guard dog.

Dog Breed Characteristics

A. Protection Ability

Bullmastiffs are endlessly loyal, and in tricky situations they will follow their owner's lead. If their owner does not accept a stranger as safe, this breed will put themselves between the owner and the threat. They will do whatever is necessary to keep their owner safe, including biting.

Score: 9/10

B. Ease of Training

Bullmastiffs can be trained, but consistency is key. Once bad habits are formed, this breed will see no reason to break them. Without puppy socialisation classes, Bullmastiffs will be aggressive towards other dogs, and to get them used to other people they should also be taken out in public throughout their life.

Score: 6/10

C. Playfulness

Despite their origins as tough guard dogs, Bullmastiffs are loyal and affectionate to their owners. They enjoy playing, but as a low-energy dog they are also perfectly content with lazing around the house.

Score: 6/10

D. Exercise needs

As a low-energy dog, Bullmastiffs only need a couple of short walks each day. Whilst they like roaming around large gardens, they are generally quite mellow.

Score: 4/10

E. Adaptability

The Bullmastiff can be left alone all day, provided there is somebody around to take them out for a toilet break. They can adapt to most weather conditions, but they do need a spacious living area. Novice owners should avoid this breed, as they require heavy-going training for their entire lives.

Score: 5/10

Dog Breed 20 - Bulldog

General Information

Dog Name: Bulldog

Dog breed Group: Companion dogs

Size Category: Large dog breeds

Height: Ranges from one foot to one foot, three inches (measured from the shoulder).

Weight: Ranges from 40 to 50 pounds

Lifespan: Ranges from 8 to 12 years.

Brief History

The origins of the Bulldog are not pretty. The breed was popular in 15th century England, where they were mostly used for the barbaric sport of bull-baiting, in which a Bulldog would latch onto a tethered bull's nose and refuse to let go until either the bull had been pulled to the ground or the Bulldog was killed. For a long time, Bulldogs were bred for pure aggression. After the bizarre sport was banned, Bulldogs were exported to the USA and Germany, where they mostly worked as herding dogs. Nowadays the Bulldog is a popular choice of mascot for many universities and sports teams, and it's also a loveable domestic pet.

Dog Breed Characteristics

A. Protection Ability

American Bulldogs retain the aggression of their ancestors, and so they make excellent guard dogs. By contrast, English Bulldogs have had the aggression bred out of them, and they are now friendly and loving. The protective ability of the Bulldog therefore depends upon their breeding.

Score: 5/10

B. Ease of Training

Bulldogs are not the most obedient dogs, but they can indeed be taught and are unlikely to forget their lessons. Bulldogs are particularly receptive to fun, repetitive dog training sessions.

Score: 6/10

C. Playfulness

Modern Bulldogs are very laid back. They enjoy playtime, but as a low-energy dog they are also content with snuggling up to their owners on the sofa.

Score: 7/10

D. Exercise needs

Bulldogs do not have much energy, but they do need at least a small amount of exercise to prevent them from becoming overweight. They tend to enjoy exercise, as it's usually quite light and followed by a nap.

Score: 4/10

E. Adaptability

Bulldogs are very easy-going, and so they can adapt to most situations. They can live in a home of any size, and love being around children. They do not adapt well to especially hot or cold weather, and so ideally they should live indoors with their owners.

Score: 7/10

Dog Breed 16-20 Quiz

The solution to this quiz can be found in *Appendix D* at the end of this book.

1. A suitable dog breed for novice owners, they can tolerate many changes to their environment. As long as they are kept warm and safe from the elements, they will be content.
   a) Dachshund
   b) Chinese Shar-Pei
   c) Bull mastiff
   d) Dalmatian

2. A formidable hunter, these tiny dogs originate from fifteenth century Germany, where their small bodies were perfect for sneaking into badger burrows and fighting them to the death. Their stubby legs made them efficient hunters, and their barks were loud enough to alert their owners when they found their prey underground.
   a) Dachshund
   b) Chinese Shar-Pei
   c) Bull dog
   d) Dalmatian

3. Impressive circus performers, this dog breed are intelligent and boast an excellent memory. No wonder they continue to thrive as firehouse dogs, coaching dogs, retrievers, among others.
   a) Dachshund
   b) Chinese Shar-Pei
   c) Bull dog
   d) Dalmatian

4. Due to their intelligence and headstrong nature, it is important that they are trained with a firm hand from an early age. Inconsistent training will lead them to believe that they are in charge.
   a) Dalmatian
   b) Chinese Shar-Pei
   c) Bull dog
   d) Bullmastiff

5. The only guard dog breed to originate from England.
   a) Dachshund
   b) Bullmastiff
   c) Bull dog
   d) Dalmatian

6. Endlessly loyal. In tricky situations, they will follow their owner's leads. If their owner does not accept a stranger as safe, this breed will put themselves between the owner and the threat. They will do whatever is necessary to keep their owner safe, including biting!
   a) Dalmatian
   b) Chinese Shar-Pei
   c) Bull dog
   d) Bullmastiff

7. A unique dog breed. Due to their intelligence and headstrong nature, it is important that they are trained with a firm hand from an early age. Inconsistent training will lead them to believe that they are in charge.
   a) Dalmatian
   b) Chinese Shar-Pei
   c) Bull dog

d) Bullmastiff

Dog Breed 21- Akita

General Information

Dog Name: Akita

Dog breed Group: Working dogs

Size Category: Large dog breeds

Height: Ranges from two feet to two feet, four inches (measured from the shoulder).

Weight: Ranges from 70 to 130 pounds.

Lifespan: Ranges from 10 to 12 years.

Brief History

The Akita can be traced back to the seventeenth century, where it had the honor of guarding Japanese royalty. It was an ideal career for the Akita, as this breed is famed for its fearlessness and devotion to its family. Perhaps the most famous member of this breed was Hachiko, a Japanese national treasure who so loved their owner that they continued to walk to his workplace every afternoon for ten years after he had passed away. After World War II many American soldiers brought Akitas back to the USA, and as the years passed the American Akita, a more robust version of the breed, grew in popularity.

Dog Breed Characteristics

A. Protection Ability

The Akita is considered to be one of the very best guard dogs. They are alert, intelligent, and they have no qualms with taking down an intruder – they even interpret prolonged eye contact as a threat.

Score: 9/10

B. Ease of Training

This is not an easy breed to train. Akitas want to be dominant, and so owners must be vigilant and firm to keep control of their pet. Even experienced dog-owners may need assistance from a professional dog trainer.

Score: 3/10

C. Playfulness

Whilst the Akita is aloof with strangers, they shower their owners in affection. They want to be involved in all family activities, and their overpowering presence can sometimes be a challenge.

Score: 8/10

D. Exercise needs

Akitas need up to an hour of daily exercise. They enjoy walking, jogging and playing in the garden, but they should always be kept on a lead when in public, as they are very aggressive towards other dogs.

Score: 7/10

E. Adaptability

Caring for an Akita is challenging. They need a large living space, hate being left alone for long periods of time and they are not stranger-friendly. Only experienced and determined owners should attempt to care for this breed.

Score: 3/10

Dog Breed 22 - Alaskan Malamute

General Information

Dog Name: Alaskan Malamute (Nickname: Mal)

Dog breed Group: Working dogs

Size Category: Large dog breeds

Height: Ranges from one foot, eleven inches to two feet, one inch (measured from the shoulder).

Weight: Ranges from 75 to 100 pounds

Lifespan: Ranges from 12 to 15 years.

Brief History

The Alaskan Malamute is thought to be the oldest breed native to North America, as well as the breed longest associated with humans. White explorers first found these dogs in Alaska, but they are undoubtedly descended from the sled dogs which took prehistoric man from Asia to Greenland thousands of years ago. The breed almost died out during the 1896 gold rush, when other sled dogs were brought to Alaska and mixed with the Alaskan Malamutes. Luckily some Mals remained and many were put to work during World War II, but the breed was thrust into peril for a second time when many of them were destroyed after serving the USA on an expedition to Antarctica.

Dog Breed Characteristics

A. Protection Ability

Despite their imposing stature, Alaskan Malamutes make terrible guard dogs. They are happy-go-lucky and have no protective instincts, and so it wouldn't occur to them that strangers shouldn't always be welcomed.

Score: 2/10

B. Ease of Training

Alaskan Malamutes are desperate for a purpose, and they love to work. Problems arise in dog training sessions when they can't see the purpose of the session – they want to be dominant, and they want to know why they're being asked to perform a task. They are, however, very intelligent and can be trained with a firm and determined owner.

Score: 6/10

C. Playfulness

Mals see everybody as a potential new friend, and their sky-high energy levels means that they are constantly playing, running and making their distinctive "woo woo" sound. This dog is not for the faint-heated; they need lots of love and lots of enthusiasm.

Score: 9/10

D. Exercise needs

Without sufficient exercise, this breed will become bored and destructive. They enjoy long walks, hiking (whilst carrying a backpack) and even skijoring (pulling a person on skis). It's very difficult to exhaust a Mal.

Score: 9/10

E. Adaptability

This breed is very sensitive and can't abide living in an apartment. They need space to roam and they need to be around their owners regularly. Unsurprisingly, they're extremely resistant to cold weather, but they enjoy life as an indoors dog. This is definitely not a breed for novice owners.

Score: 3/10

Dog Breed 23 - Afghan Hound

General Information

Dog Name: Afghan Hound

Dog breed Group: Hound dogs

Size Category: Large dog breeds

Height: Ranges from two feet to two feet, four inches (measured from the shoulder).

Weight: Ranges from 50 to 60 pounds.

Lifespan: Ranges from 10 to 12 years.

Brief History

This distinctive breed is both agile and gentle, making them an excellent hunter and shepherd in their native Afghanistan. The Afghan Hound is thought to have existed for thousands of years but didn't leave the country until the early twentieth century, when they were brought to the UK and USA as potential show dogs. The breed's popularity skyrocketed in the 1970s, when the Afghan Hound was introduced as Barbie's newest pet.

Dog Breed Characteristics

A. Protection Ability

This breed is an excellent watchdog. They are fiercely protective of their owners, and their loud bark is usually enough to spook intruders.

Score: 7/10

B. Ease of Training

Afghan Hounds learn slowly, possibly due to their stubborn nature. In terms of temperament this breed is more cat than dog, and will often completely ignore commands. This is perhaps one of the most difficult breeds to train.

Score: 1/10

C. Playfulness

This breed is often described as aloof, but in truth they are very loyal to their owners. They are not the most affectionate dogs, but will often act the clown and engage in play.

Score: 6/10

D. Exercise needs

Afghan Hounds need a fair amount of exercise each day. They enjoy walks and romping in the garden, though it should be noted that they can jump exceptionally high - owners should invest in a high fence.

Score: 7/10

E. Adaptability

The Afghan Hound is comfortable in all weathers, and will happily live in an apartment. Whilst they can be a challenge to train, they are generally quite easy to handle and are suitable for novice owners.

Score: 8/10

Dog Breed 24 - Australian Cattle Dog

General Information

Dog Name: Australian Cattle Dog

Dog breed Group: Herding dogs

Size Category: Medium-sized dog breeds

Height: Ranges from one foot, five inches to one foot, eight inches (measured from the shoulder).

Weight: Ranges from 30 to 50 pounds

Lifespan: Ranges from 12 to 15 years.

Brief History

The Australian Cattle Dog is a relatively new breed, and so it's surprising that nobody knows exactly which breeds were mixed to achieve this breed. Early settlers of Australia brought with them an English dog, the Smithfield, to herd cattle, but they soon decided that this rough and noisy breed was unsuited to the job. Through lots of experimentation, the Australian Cattle Dog was finally bred. It truly is the perfect herding dog for the outback; it can work silently, but is firm enough to get the job done.

Dog Breed Characteristics

A. Protection Ability

The Australian Cattle Dog is an imposing figure that will intimidate even the toughest of intruders. Constantly alert and ready to bark, this breed is an excellent watchdog.

Score: 7/10

B. Ease of Training

The most important part of training an Australian Cattle Dog is to establish the owner as the alpha. Dog training is particularly important with this breed, as they tend to nip, and this habit must be discouraged before it becomes dangerous. Once a clear hierarchy is demonstrated, this breed will be relatively easy to train.

Score: 8/10

C. Playfulness

Temperament can vary widely across this breed, but as a rule Australian Cattle Dogs are very attached to their owners, so much so that they consider isolation to be a punishment. Whilst not the most affectionate of breeds, Australian Cattle Dogs love their owners and are endlessly loyal.

Score: 5/10

D. Exercise needs

The Australian Cattle Dog was bred to herd and chase, and so this is exactly what they do. They need lots of daily exercise, and they will chase anything that moves.

Score: 9/10

E. Adaptability

This breed needs a large living space – it has too much energy for an apartment! They are very rambunctious and require an experienced dog owner.

Score: 4/10

Dog Breed 25 - Basenji

General Information

Dog Name: Basenji

Dog breed Group: Hound dog

Size Category: Small dog breeds

Height: Ranges from one foot, four inches to one foot, five inches (measured from the shoulder).

Weight: Ranges from 22 to 24 pounds.

Lifespan: Ranges from 10 to 12 years.

Brief History

The Basenji's name translates to "small wild thing from the bush", but in truth this breed is quiet and calculated. This ancient breed originates from Central Africa, where they lived in the own communities alongside pygmy tribes for centuries. Basenjis weren't discovered by Westerners until the 19th century, and they were quickly put to work as hunting dogs. Their skill was so great that some African tribes valued a good hunting Basenji over a wife. Nowadays the breed is rare, although there are some Basenjis in the UK and USA.

Dog Breed Characteristics

A. Protection Ability

Basenjis are suspicious of strangers, and extremely protective of their owners, and so they are good watch dogs. Whilst they are wary of strangers they won't attack, and so they are poor guard dogs.

Score: 6/10

B. Ease of Training

This Basenji is very stubborn and unreceptive to dog training, perhaps due to the thousands of years the breed spent living without human interaction. Owners often find it easiest to hire an experienced dog trainer to tame their Basenji.

Score: 2/10

C. Playfulness

This breed is not at all playful. They are curious and energetic, but they do not need much affection from their owners.

Score: 3/10

D. Exercise needs

As a hunting dog, the Basenji needs lots of exercise. Whilst some are content with a daily walk, others will have enough energy to tear apart their owners' homes.

Score: 9/10

E. Adaptability

The Basenji is adaptable in most respects, its only sticking point is that it cannot abide cold weather and is very much an indoors dog. It will be happy in any type of home, and is happy to be left alone for long periods of time.

Score: 8/10

Dog Breed 21-25 Quiz

The solution to this quiz can be found in *Appendix E* at the end of this book.

1. Bred for its fearlessness and devotion to its family, this dog breed's history can be traced back to the seventeenth century, where it had the honour of guarding Japanese royalty.
   a) Basenji
   b) Akita
   c) Alaskan Malamute
   d) Afghan Hound

2. This is not an easy breed to train. They want to be dominant, and so owners must be vigilant and firm to keep control of their pet. Strangers beware, this dog breed often interprets prolonged eye contact as a threat
   a) Afghan Hound
   b) Akita
   c) Alaskan Malamute
   d) Basenji

3. This dog breed is believed to have descended from the sled dogs which took prehistoric man from Asia to Greenland thousands of years ago. Many of them perished after serving the USA on an expedition to Antarctica.
   a) Afghan Hound
   b) Akita
   c) Alaskan Malamute
   d) Basenji

4. Despite their imposing stature, they make terrible guard dogs. They are happy-go-lucky and have no protective instincts, and so it wouldn't occur to them that strangers shouldn't always be welcomed
   a) Akita

b) Alaskan Malamute
c) Australian Cattle dog
d) Basenji

5. This dog breeds popularity skyrocketed in the 1970s when it was introduced as Barbie's newest pet.
   a) Afghan Hound
   b) Akita
   c) Alaskan Malamute
   d) Basenji

6. Perhaps one of the most difficult breeds to train, this dog breed learns slowly. With regards to their temperament they are more cat than dog, and will often completely ignore commands.
   a) Afghan Hound
   b) Akita
   c) Australian Cattle Dog
   d) Basenji

7. This dog breed is very stubborn and unreceptive to dog training, perhaps due to the thousands of years the breed spent living without human interaction. Owners often find it easiest to hire an experienced dog trainer to train them.
   a) Afghan Hound
   b) Akita
   c) Australian Cattle Dog
   d) Basenji

Dog Breed 26 - Beagle

General Information

Dog Name: Beagle

Dog breed Group: Hound dogs

Size Category: Small dog breeds

Height: Ranges from one foot, one inch to one foot, three inches (measured at the shoulder).

Weight: Ranges from 18 to 30 pounds.

Lifespan: Ranges from 10 to 15 years.

Brief History

The Beagle is has a varied history. It's theorized that these small dogs originated in Greece at around 400BC, but it is since their arrival in England that the breed has undergone the most changes. Since the fourteenth century the breed has taken on many forms including the extra-tiny Glove Beagle, the Pocket Beagle, the loud-mouthed Singing Beagle and the colorful Patch Beagle. In the eighteenth century the Foxhound overtook the Beagle as the hunting dog of choice, and so they were relegated working on farms around the UK. Nowadays, the Beagle is a popular companion dog in the UK and USA.

Dog Breed Characteristics

A. Protection Ability

Beagles are not aggressive dogs. They have no protective instinct and they are not visually intimidating. It is therefore unsurprising that they do not make the best guard dogs or watch dogs.

Score: 2/10

B. Ease of Training

Whilst traditional dog training techniques do not work with Beagles, they can indeed be trained. With a little determination and creativity, owners should be able to train their Beagle without too many issues.

Score: 6/10

C. Playfulness

Young Beagles are extremely playful and attached to their owners. As they get older, Beagles become a little bit lazier and will be content to laze around the house for most of the day.

Score: 6/10

D. Exercise needs

This breed is prone to obesity, and so it's important that owners get their Beagles to exercise. They are generally lively and energetic enough that when prompted, they will indeed exercise.

Score: 8/10

E. Adaptability

Beagles are happy living in large houses or small apartments, and they are very friendly to all they encounter. They cannot abide being alone for long periods of time, and may shiver during cold weather.

Score: 5/10

Dog Breed 27 - Bedlington Terrier

General Information

Dog Name: Bedlington Terrier

Dog breed Group: Terrier dogs

Size Category: Small dog breeds

Height: Ranges from one foot, three inches to one foot, four inches (measured from the shoulder).

Weight: Ranges from 17 to 23 pounds.

Lifespan: Ranges from 14 to 16 years.

Brief History

As the name suggests, the Bedlington Terrier first became known in Bedlington, a town in the north of England. Prior to its arrival in the UK, it's thought that this breed was travelling across Europe with bands of gypsies, who kept them around to kill small vermin such as badgers and rats. Bedlington Terriers are fast runners, and English factory workers would often race them against Whippets (a similarly quick breed). In the early twentieth century it became fashionable to trim the Bedlington Terrier's fur in the distinctive way which is now so recognizable.

Dog Breed Characteristics

A. Protection Ability

Bedlington Terriers are constantly alert and are reasonably intelligent. These traits make them good watch dogs, and they will loudly alert their owners to any unusual goings on.

Score: 7/10

B. Ease of Training

This breed can be trained, but it's important that they believe that the tasks are beneficial to them in some way – they can be very stubborn. With a skilled trainer, this breed can be successfully trained to obedience.

Score: 7/10

C. Playfulness

The Bedlington Terrier is an affectionate, gentle breed which adores playing with their owners and young children. Whilst they can be aggressive towards other dogs, this instinct doesn't extend to humans.

Score: 8/10

D. Exercise needs

As high-energy dogs, Bedlington Terriers spend most of each day running and staying active. They enjoy daily walks and will chase smaller animals if given the chance.

Score: 7/10

E. Adaptability

This is a relatively easy breed for the novice owner. They are happy living in a variety of settings, are great with children and can be left alone throughout the day.

Score: 9/10

Dog Breed 28 - Belgian Malinois

General Information

Dog Name: Belgian Malinois (Nickname: Maline)

Dog breed Group: Herding dogs

Size Category: Large dog breeds

Height: Ranges from one foot, ten inches to two feet, two inches (measured from the shoulder).

Weight: Ranges from 40 to 80 pounds.

Lifespan: Ranges from 12 to 14 years.

Brief History

The Belgian Malinois is one of four breeds of sheepdog that were developed in nineteenth century Belgium. In the early twentieth century the breed became popular at dog shows in Belgium, where they performed better than most other sheepdogs. The breed went on to work in several roles during World War I, as messenger dogs, Red Cross dogs and light machine gun cart dogs. After the war many soldiers brought these dogs home with them, and the breed began to gain popularity in the USA and Europe. Nowadays the Belgian Malinois is highly respected for their careers in the military and with the police force.

Dog Breed Characteristics

A. Protection Ability

The military and police force consider this breed to be one of the top guard dogs around. With its strong yet light build and high intelligence, the Belgian Malinois will put up a fierce fight – it is a force to be reckoned with.

Score: 9/10

B. Ease of Training

The Belgian Malinois is intelligent, agile, and a quick learner. They do very well in a range of activities, including tracking, herding, flyball and obedience. They are eager to please and so dog training is typically a breeze.

Score: 8/10

C. Playfulness

These dogs have a high play drive, which means that they love to play, and always have time for their owners. They're very affectionate with their owners, and particularly enjoy playing with kids.

Score: 9/10

D. Exercise needs

The Belgian Malinois needs twenty minutes of exercise at least three or four times a day. A relaxing stroll isn't going to cut it – this breed needs to be active, and the best way to exercise them is to play games or sports with them.

Score: 9/10

E. Adaptability

As long as this breed has room to roam, they will be happy. They are comfortable in any type of weather, and can spend periods of time alone. Novice owners can take on this breed, provided they have the energy and determination that the Belgian Malinois needs from an owner.

Score: 7/10

Dog Breed 29 - Belgian Sheepdog

General Information

Dog Name: Belgian Sheepdog

Dog breed Group: Herding dogs

Size Category: Large dog breeds

Height: Ranges from one foot, ten inches to two feet, two inches (measured from the shoulder).

Weight: Ranges from 60 to 75 pounds.

Lifespan: Ranges from 10 to 12 years.

Brief History

The Belgian Sheepdog first emerged in nineteenth century Belgium. Despite their name, this breed is so much more than a sheepdog. They can be easily trained into a number of careers; over the last couple of centuries this breed has excelled in border patrols, battlefields and police forces around the world. Modern Belgian Sheepdogs can be found working in search and rescue, as guide dogs for the blind and as service dogs for the disabled.

Dog Breed Characteristics

A. Protection Ability

Belgian Sheepdogs are suspicious of strangers and protective of their families, which make them very good watchdogs. They also be aggressive when necessary, and so they also make good guard dogs.

Score: 8/10

B. Ease of Training

This breed is highly intelligence and responsive to training, but they are also independent thinkers. For dog training to be a success, owners must earn their dogs trust and respect without the use of force – Belgian Sheepdogs are very sensitive, and a heavy hand can permanently damage their temperament.

Score: 8/10

C. Playfulness

This breed is affectionate and protective of their owners' children, whom they view as their own. They must be supervised when in public because they can often interpret loud noises as a threat to "their" children, and they will attack. They are very energetic, and usually ready to play.

Score: 9/10

D. Exercise needs

This breed needs at least an hour of exercise each day, and they particularly enjoy retrieval games. They also enjoy accompanying their owners on hikes or other outdoor activities – as long as they're busy, the Belgian Sheepdog is happy!

Score: 9/10

E. Adaptability

The main challenge with this breed is their sensitivity, but this can be helped with training. They can live in a variety of environments and weather conditions, and great with children.

Score: 7/10

Dog Breed 30 - Bichon Frise

General Information

Dog Name: Bichon Frise

Dog breed Group: Companion dogs

Size Category: Small dog breeds

Height: Ranges from nine inches to eleven inches (measured from the shoulder).

Weight: Ranges from 7 to 12 pounds.

Lifespan: Ranges from 12 to 15 years.

Brief History

The earliest known instance of the Bichon Frise was in the fourteenth century, when French sailors brought them home with them from Tenerife. These fluffy little dogs instantly became beloved companions to European royals – King Henry III loved his Bichon Frises so much that he carried them everywhere with him in a special basket which hung from his neck. Sadly this popularity didn't last, and by the nineteenth century the breed was more commonly seen with organ grinders and street performers. Nowadays, the Bichon Frise is a beloved family pet to millions across Europe and the USA.

Dog Breed Characteristics

A. Protection Ability

The Bichon Frise is simply too laid back to be an effective protector. With virtually no aggressive or protective tendencies, this breed is much more suited to lazing inside the house rather than protecting it.

Score: 2/10

B. Ease of Training

This breed is intelligent and eager to please. They perform very well with obedience training, and are particularly talented at tricks and canine sports.

Score: 8/10

C. Playfulness

The Bichon Frise relishes being the centre of attention, and they are known for their cheerful disposition. Always ready to play, this breed is particularly suited to families with young children.

Score: 8/10

D. Exercise needs

Whilst this breed is primarily an indoor dog, they have lots of energy and should exercise daily. This can often be accomplished through play. If they don't get enough exercise, these dogs will become destructive.

Score: 7/10

E. Adaptability

This breed can adapt to most situations, but it cannot abide being alone and often suffers separation anxiety. Bichon Frises should only be cared for by owners who have the time and energy to spend an awful lot of time with them!

Score: 7/10

Dog Breed 26-30 Quiz

The solution to this quiz can be found in *Appendix F* at the end of this book.

1. This dog breed is particularly prone to obesity, and so it's important that their owners get them to exercise. They are generally lively and energetic enough that when prompted, they will indeed exercise
   a) Bichon Frise
   b) Bedlington Terrier
   c) Beagle
   d) Belgian Malinois

2. It is thought that this breed travelled across Europe with bands of gypsies, who kept them around to kill small vermins such as badgers and rats. They are particularly fast runners.
   a) Bichon Frise
   b) Bedlington Terrier
   c) Beagle
   d) Belgian Malinois

3. It is thought that this breed travelled across Europe with bands of gypsies, who kept them around to kill small vermins such as badgers and rats. They are particularly fast runners, gentle, affectionate and are happy living in a variety of settings – an ideal breed for the novice owner.
   a) Bichon Frise
   b) Bedlington Terrier
   c) Beagle
   d) Belgian Malinois

4. The military and police force consider this breed to be one of the top guard dogs around. With its strong yet light build and high intelligence, this dog breed will put up a fight – it is a force to be reckoned with.
   a) Bichon Frise
   b) Bedlington Terrier
   c) Beagle
   d) Belgian Malinois

5. This dog breed is intelligent, agile and a quick learner. They do well in a range of activities, including tracking, herding, flying and obedience. They are eager to please and so dog training is typically a breeze.
   a) Bichon Frise
   b) Belgian Malinois
   c) Bedlington Terrier
   d) Beagle

6. Simply too laid back to be an effective protector, this dog breed virtually has no aggressive or protective tendencies. Its much more suited to lazing inside the house rather than protecting it.
   a) Bichon Frise
   b) Bedlington Terrier
   c) Beagle
   d) Belgian Malinois

7. Well loved by European royals, this dog breed has a history with King Henry III. He loved his dogs so much that he carried them everywhere with him in a special basket, which hung from his neck!
   a) Bichon Frise
   e) Bedlington Terrier

f) Beagle

g) Belgian Malinois

8. Known for their cheerful disposition, this dog breed relishes being the centre of attention. Always ready to play, they are particularly suited to families with young children.

   a) Belgian Sheepdog

   b) Bedlington Terrier

   c) Bichon Frise

   d) Belgian Malinois

Dog Breed 31 - Bernese Mountain Dog

General Information

Dog Name: Bernese Mountain Dog (Nickname: Berner).

Dog breed Group: Working dogs

Size Category: Large dog breeds

Height: Ranges from one foot, eleven inches to two feet, three inches (measured from the shoulder).

Weight: Ranges from 70 to 115 pounds.

Lifespan: Ranges from 6 to 8 years.

Brief History

By the end of the nineteenth century the Bernese Mountain Dog was on the brink of extinction – originally brought to Switzerland by the Romans, they were used a general purpose dogs and little attention was paid to preserving the breed. If it hadn't been for a small group of Swiss breeders, the Bernese Mountain dog may have disappeared completely. Soon after the breed was developed (and named after the town of Bern, where these developments took place), the dogs were exhibited at dog shows around Switzerland and were soon brought to the USA.

Dog Breed Characteristics

A. Protection Ability

Bernese Mountain Dogs will bark and growl to ward off strangers, but they generally won't bite or become aggressive. They are excellent watch dogs, but simply don't have the attack instinct needed to be a guard dog.

Score: 7/10

B. Ease of Training

Intelligent and energetic, Bernese Mountain Dogs are quite easy to train. It's worth noting, however, that this breed reaches physical maturity long before they reach mental maturity, and so it's important for owners to be patient when training this breed.

Score: 8/10

C. Playfulness

The Berner is a gentle giant who loves playing with their family. Their size means that they may need extra training to teach them how to behave indoors, as in their excitement they can often end up wrecking entire rooms. This breed is never short on energy and always ready to play!

Score: 8/10

D. Exercise needs

As a working dog, the Berner needs lots of daily exercise. A minimum of 30 minutes and maximum of 90 minutes should keep this breed content.

Score: 9/10

E. Adaptability

Bernese Mountain Dogs need a lot of space, ideally in a large home with a fenced garden. They're highly sensitive (especially to hot weather) and cannot be left alone for long periods of time. This breed will be a challenge to anyone, and to especially novice owners.

Score: 3/10

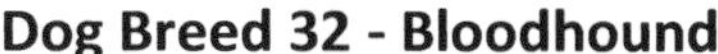

Dog Breed 32 - Bloodhound

General Information

Dog Name: Bloodhound

Dog breed Group: Hound dogs

Size Category: Large dog breeds

Height: Ranges from one foot, eleven inches to two feet, three inches (measured from the shoulder).

Weight: Ranges from 80 to 110 pounds.

Lifespan: Ranges from 11 to 15 years.

Brief History

The Bloodhound is an ancient dog breed that can be traced back to the third century, most likely to the Mediterranean. The Bloodhound came to England with William the Conquerer in 1066, where hunters quickly discovered the breed's incredible sense of smell. For many years the Bloodhound was put to work following the scent of wounded deer and wolves, until hunters became more interested in tracking speedy animals such as foxes. The bumbling Bloodhound was replaced by the swift Foxhound, and instead went on to track thieves and poachers. The breed was highly sought-after; Queen Victoria owned a pet Bloodhound, and Benjamin Franklin also expressed interest in the breed. Nowadays the breed is rather uncommon, and mostly finds work in search and rescue.

Dog Breed Characteristics

A. Protection Ability

The Bloodhound has many talents, but protection is not one of them. It's possible to train them to be passable watch dogs, but they're not nearly aggressive enough to be guard dogs.

Score: 4/10

B. Ease of Training

This breed can be trained quite easily. By nature they are curious, and so crate training is recommended for owners who want to keep their Bloodhound out of their personal belongings when left alone.

Score: 7/10

C. Playfulness

Bloodhounds can vary widely, but generally speaking they are docile and affectionate. They will play with their owners, but they are not terribly energetic and certainly won't be bouncing off the walls.

Score: 6/10

D. Exercise needs

Bloodhounds can walk for miles, and also enjoy tracking activities. Owners should take extra care to notice their dog's signs of fatigues, as it's important to not exhaust this breed.

Score: 7/10

E. Adaptability

Bloodhounds are very sensitive and will be best-suited to experienced dog owners. They need a large fenced garden to roam about in, and they do not enjoy being left alone for long periods of time.

Score: 4/10

Dog Breed 33 - Border Collie

General Information

Dog Name: Border Collie

Dog breed Group: Herding dogs

Size Category: Small dog breeds
Height: Ranges from one foot, six inches to one foot, ten inches (measured from the shoulder).

Weight: Ranges from 30 to 45 pounds.

Lifespan: Ranges from 12 to 15 years.

Brief History

The Border Collie gets its name from its place of origin: the border between England and Scotland. This breed is quite unusual, in that all members of the breed can be traced back to a single tri-colour dog called Old Hemp, who was known as the best herding dog in the area. Old Hemp rose to fame in the early twentieth century as an impressive show dog, and thus interest in the breed surged. Today, Border Collies still work as herding dogs, and are also a popular choice for a household pet.

Dog Breed Characteristics

A. Protection Ability

Border Collies have no qualms with barking loudly to alert their owners to suspicious strangers, but they will generally not attack. They are therefore very effective watch dogs, but poor guard dogs.

Score: 6/10

B. Ease of Training

This breed is intelligent and very sensitive to their owners' actions – this makes them very easy to train. They are strong-minded but ultimately want to please, and so dog training usually runs smoothly with the Border Collie.

Score: 8/10

C. Playfulness

Border Collies have loads of energy, and they love their families. They're very playful and particularly enjoy rigorous outdoor games such as frisbee or fetch. This breed can be difficult to keep up with!

Score: 9/10

D. Exercise needs

Border Collies need lots of mental and physical stimulation every day. They enjoy dog sports, brisk walks and roaming in parks. They have an instinct to chase and herd, and so owners must keep an eye of them when out in public or near roads.

Score: 9/10

E. Adaptability

The main thing a Border Collie needs from its owner is love and energy. Provided they have these core things, they will be happy regardless of their living situation.

Score: 8/10

Dog Breed 34 - Greyhound

General Information

Dog Name: Greyhound

Dog breed Group: Hound dogs

Size Category: Large dog breeds

Height: Ranges from two feet, one inch to two feet, six inches (measured from the shoulder).

Weight: Ranges from 50 to 85 pounds

Lifespan: Ranges from 12 to 15 years.

Brief History

The Greyhound is sleek, streamlined and iconic. Images of this elegant breed can be seen in paintings, pottery and literature dating back centuries, and they are thought to have existed for four thousand years. The Greyhound is set apart from other hound dogs, as it hunts visually rather than by using scent, and it can see distances up to half a mile. The exact origins of this breed are unknown, but traces of the Greyhound can be seen throughout history; as a beloved companion to Eyptian Pharaohs, a discerning pet in Homer's Odyssey, and the breed even earns a mention in The Bible. Modern day Greyhounds are most well-known for being race dogs – a controversial career, as many dogs involved in the sport end up euthenized or abandoned when they fail to excel.

Dog Breed Characteristics

A. Protection Ability

Despite their imposing stature, Greyhounds scare very easily and they're prone to running away from intruders. They are far too docile to offer their owners any protection.

Score: 2/10

B. Ease of Training

It's relatively easy to train a Greyhound, but they can be stubborn and best results can be achieved through edible rewards. They struggle with the "sit" command as it's not a natural position for them, but they will do their best to comply (often using their tail for balance).

Score: 7/10

C. Playfulness

Whilst Greyhounds tend to be aloof with strangers, they can easily be won over with treats. They are friendly and playful, but they're also prone to bouts of shyness.

Score: 6/10

D. Exercise needs

Surprisingly, the Greyhound is quite a low-energy breed. They should have at least one walk per day, and owners should watch them carefully to ensure they don't become overweight.

Score: 5/10

E. Adaptability

Greyhounds are family dogs and cannot stand being left alone for long periods of time. They're also intolerant of cold weather, and may need extra layers in the winter. This is a tricky breed that may be best suited to an experienced dog owner.

Score: 6/10

Dog Breed 35 - Great Dane

General Information

Dog Name: Great Dane

Dog breed Group: Working dogs

Size Category: Large dog breeds

Height: Ranges from two feet, four inches to two feet, ten inches (measured from the shoulder).

Weight: Ranges from 100 to 200 pounds.

Lifespan: Ranges from 7 to 10 years.

Brief History

Contrary to its name, paintings and literature suggest that the Great Dane may have its roots in ancient Egypt or China. These past versions of the Great Dane were more muscular and ferocious than the modern breed, and it is thought that the Great Dane as we know it has been bred for approximately four hundred years. The breed was developed in Germany, where it hunted wild boars (the most vicious of all large game in Europe). They then rose in popularity, becoming guard dogs for European noblemen and later was named the National Dog of Germany in 1876. The modern Great Dane is more placid than their ancestors, and is commonly a companion dog.

Dog Breed Characteristics

A. Protection Ability

Great Danes will scare away intruders with their terrifying bark, but generally will not attack. They therefore make good watch dogs, but they aren't suitable as guard dogs.

Score: 8/10

B. Ease of Training

This breed is moderately intelligent and receptive to dog training. They are commonly crate trained, as their large size can lead to mishaps around the house when their owner is absent.

Score: 8/10

C. Playfulness

The Great Dane is energetic and eager to please - they would play all day if given the chance! They're also very friendly towards children and enjoy showing them affection.

Score: 9/10

D. Exercise needs

This breed is full of energy, and will become destructive if they don't get enough daily exercise. They may even need up to one hour of rigorous running per day.

Score: 9/10

E. Adaptability

This is a challenging breed, even for experienced owners. They need lots of space due to their size, and cannot tolerate being alone. Despite their size, they are also very sensitive to the cold.

Score: 3/10

Dog Breed 31-35 Quiz

The solution to this quiz can be found in *Appendix G* at the end of this book.

1. This dog breed was brought to Switzerland by the Romans who used them as general purpose dogs.
   a) Bloodhound
   b) Great Dane
   c) Bernese mountain dog
   d) Greyhound

2. Intelligent and energetic, this dog breed is quite easy to train. It's worth noting, however, that this breed reaches physical maturity long before they reach mental maturity, and so it's important for owners to be patient when training them.
   a) Bloodhound
   b) Bernese mountain dog
   c) Border Collie
   d) Greyhound

3. Equipped with an incredible sense of smell, this dog breed came to England with William the Conqueror in 1066.
   a) Bloodhound
   b) Great Dane
   c) Bernese mountain dog
   d) Greyhound

4. Although this dog breed can vary widely, generally speaking they are docile and affectionate. They will play with their owners, but they are not terribly energetic and certainly won't be bouncing off the walls.
   a) Great Dane
   b) Bloodhound

c) Border Collie

d) Bernese mountain dog

5. This dog breed gets it's name from its place of origin: the border between England and Scotland

a) Great Dane

b) Bloodhound

c) Border Collie

d) Bernese mountain dog

6. This dog breed has loads of energy, and they love their families. They're very playful and particularly enjoy rigorous outdoor games such as Frisbee or fetch. This breed can be difficult to keep up with!

a) Border Collie

b) Bloodhound

c) Great Dane

d) Greyhound

7. This dog breed needs lots of mental and physical stimulation every day. They enjoy dog sports, brisk walks and roaming in parks. They have an instinct to chase and herd, and so owners must keep an eye of them when out in public or near roads.

a) Great Dane

b) Bloodhound

c) Border Collie

d) Bernese mountain dog

8. Sleek, streamlined and iconic. This dog breed is set apart from other hound dogs, as it hunts visually rather than by using scent, and it can see distances up to half a mile!

a) Great Dane

b) Bloodhound

c) Greyhound

d) Border Collie

9. Despite their imposing stature, this dog breed scare very easily and they're prone to running away from intruders. They are far too docile to offer their owners any protection.

   a) Great Dane

   b) Bloodhound

   c) Border Collie

   d) Greyhound

10. This dog breed will scare away intruders with their terrifying bark, but generally will not attack. They therefore make good watch dogs, but they aren't suitable as guard dogs.

    a) Great Dane

    b) Bloodhound

    c) Border Collie

    d) Bernese mountain dog

Dog Breed 36 - Great Pyrenees

General Information

Dog Name: Great Pyrenees (Nickname: Pyr)

Dog breed Group: Working dogs

Size Category: Large dog breeds

Height: Ranges from two feet, one inch to two feet, eight inches (measured from the shoulder).

Weight: Ranges from 85 to 160 pounds.

Lifespan: Ranges from 10 to 12 years.

Brief History

The Great Pyrenees is an impressive dog breed with a humble beginning. It's thought to have originated over ten thousand years ago in Asia Minor, when shepherds decided that they needed canine assistance. Originally owned by peasants, the Great Pyrenees eventually caught the eye of the monarchy, and in 1675 it was named the Royal Dog of France. This title proved the catalyst for the Great Pyrenees, as they were soon being exported to North America and all over Europe. The breed suffered during the two World Wars, but nowadays it has been restored to its former glory.

Dog Breed Characteristics

A. Protection Ability

The Great Pyrenees was bred to guard flocks, and they have retained this protective instinct. They are typically placid until provoked, and they can put up an intimidating fight against intruders.

Score: 7/10

B. Ease of Training

The Pyr is a large dog and so absolutely needs to be trained. They are very intuitive and have an excellent memory, but dog training can be difficult due to their overly sensitive nature. This breed responds well to gentle, positive reinforcement – they will quickly shut down and become timid when trained harshly.

Score: 4/10

C. Playfulness

This breed can seem quite sober at times, as they enjoy spending time alone and are very docile. They are very affectionate to their owners (in fact, they are a popular choice of therapy dog), and despite their size Pyrs are very gentle. Whilst they aren't the most energetically playful breed, there is no doubt that they will make their owners feel their love.

Score: 7/10

D. Exercise needs

This breed needs at least 30 minutes of exercise each day (quite a small amount for a dog of their size). They love hiking and will cheerfully carry backpacks and supplies for their owners, but extra caution must be taken during hot weather to ensure they don't overheat.

Score: 6/10

E. Adaptability

The Great Pyrenees is likely to be too challenging for first-time owners. They need lots of space in which to roam around, and due to their size they are prone to exhaustion in the summer. Ideally, Pyrs need attentive, energetic owners who can give them the unique style of care they require.

Score: 4/10

Dog Breed 37 - Gordon Setter

General Information

Dog Name: Gordon Setter

Dog breed Group: Sporting dogs

Size Category: Large dog breeds

Height: Ranges from one foot, eleven inches to two feet, three inches (measured from the shoulder).

Weight: Ranges from 45 to 80 pounds.

Lifespan: Ranges from 10 to 12 years.

Brief History

The Gordon Setter is a steady and calculated hunter. Originally from Scotland, this breed air scents its prey and is known for rarely making errors. They get their name from the fourth Duke of Gordon, who was a fan of the breed and brought them to prominence. The first Gordon Setters to make it to the USA came from the Duke's personal kennels. Nowadays these dogs are a popular choice of companion in the USA, and the Gordon Setter Club of America has over one thousand members.

Dog Breed Characteristics

A. Protection Ability

This breed is very disciplined, and in addition to be an excellent hunter they also perform well as both a watch dog and a guard dog.

Score: 7/10

B. Ease of Training

The Gordon Setter is very receptive to dog training, but their high intelligence means that they will sometimes attempt to take advantage of their owners. Effective owners must be firm and establish themselves as the leader in order to get the most out of their pets.

Score: 9/10

C. Playfulness

Despite their innate sense of discipline, this breed has a huge capacity for playfulness. They enjoy being around their owners and are always ready to show affection.

Score: 8/10

D. Exercise needs

Gordon Setters require rigorous daily exercise, and they're the perfect companion for joggers. Forced exercise such as road running and obedience jumps should be phased into their routine after they have reached two years of age, as this sort of exercise can put a heavy strain on their developing joints.

Score: 8/10

E. Adaptability

Gordon Setters can adapt to most living environments, but they hate being alone for long periods of time. Novice owners can take on this breed, provided they're prepared for a challenge!

Score: 7/10

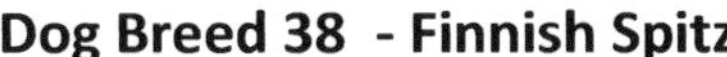

Dog Breed 38 - Finnish Spitz

General Information

Dog Name: Finnish Spitz

Dog breed Group: Sporting dogs

Size Category: Small dog breeds

Height: Ranges from one foot, three inches to one foot, eight inches (measured form the shoulder).

Weight: Ranges from 20 to 35 pounds.

Lifespan: Ranges from 12 to 15 years.

Brief History

At first glance, it would be easy to underestimate the petite Finnish Spitz, but in truth these dogs are skilled hunters, taking down everything from squirrels to bears. As European clans travelled across the continent thousands of years ago, the purebred Finnish Spitz was crossed with breed after breed in an attempt to alter its skills to suit the geography of each new area. By 1880 the breed was approaching extinction, until Hugo Roos (a pioneer in this breed) took the initiative to travel across Scandinavia, finding purebreeds and salvaging the Finnish Spitz. In the twentieth century the breed was brought to the USA and UK, where it remains today as a sturdy worker and companion.

Dog Breed Characteristics

A. Protection Ability

Constantly alert, the Finnish Spitz is a decent watch dog that can bark up to 160 times a minute. Its distinctive yodelling bark is enough to scare away any intruder.

Score: 8/10

B. Ease of Training

The Finnish Spitz is fiercely independent and become easily bored with repetitive training sessions. The best approach to use with this breed is one of calm assertiveness and strong (but not harsh) leadership. Make no mistakes: dog training is a challenge with this breed.

Score: 3/10

C. Playfulness

This active little dog is highly affectionate and attached to the people they love. They have lots of energy and love nothing more than playing with their owners, especially young children.

Score: 9/10

D. Exercise needs

The Finnish Spitz is strong willed and needs lots of exercise each day. This breed isn't recommended for people who work long days or live in apartments, as the breed can be very demanding. Without sufficient daily exercise the Finnish Spitz will resort to digging, hunting, or its trademark barking.

Score: 8/10

E. Adaptability

With its separation anxiety, high energy, persistent barking and resistance to training, this breed can certainly be a challenge! The Finnish Spitz is best suited to an enthusiastic, patient owner.

Score: 4/10

Dog Breed 39 - Field Spaniel

General Information

Dog Name: Field Spaniel

Dog breed Group: Sporting dogs

Size Category: Medium dog breeds

Height: Ranges from one foot, four inches to one foot, seven inches (measured form the shoulder).

Weight: Ranges from 37 to 45 pounds.

Lifespan: Ranges from 10 to 12 years.

Brief History

The Field Spaniel originates from nineteenth century England, where it was used for hunting birds and small animals. It was considered to be the same breed as the English Cocker Spaniel until the early twentieth century, when it was decided that dogs weighing over 25 pounds would be considered a Field Spaniel. This breed is extremely rare, most likely due to the immense popularity of the English Cocker Spaniel.

Dog Breed Characteristics

A. Protection Ability

These are placid dogs that wouldn't think to attack an intruder. They are, however, effective watch dogs who maintain a state of alertness and will bark a warning to strangers.

Score: 5/10

B. Ease of Training

The Field Spaniel is eager to please, and its origins as a hunter and watch dog means that it is disciplined and receptive to training. This breed is very easy to train, and if given the chance they will stand out from the crowd in obedience tasks.

Score: 8/10

C. Playfulness

Field Spaniels can be reserved with strangers, but they shower their owners in love. They are playful and gentle, especially with children. They prefer quiet play to rough and tumble.

Score: 6/10

D. Exercise needs

This breed is moderately active, and likes to run throughout the day. They're natural explorers and will occasionally follow their nose rather than their owner's commands. Field Spaniels have lots of energy and owners should walk this breed at least once a day.

Score: 7/10

E. Adaptability

This breed has too much energy for apartment living and they're reluctant to spend much time alone. With a bit of research and determination, novice owners can handle this breed.

Score: 6/10

Dog Breed 40 - Brittany

General Information

Dog Name: Brittany

Dog breed Group: Sporting dogs

Size Category: Medium dog breeds

Height: Ranges from one foot, five inches to one foot, eight inches (measured from the shoulder).

Weight: Ranges from 30 to 40 pounds.

Lifespan: Ranges from 10 to 13 years.

Brief History

As the name suggests, the Brittany hails from Brittany, in the north-west of France. The breed can be seen in paintings from the seventeenth century, but its exact origins are uncertain. Brittanys were very sought after in nineteenth century France due to their impressive pointer and setter abilities, and their willingness to follow orders made them the perfect assistant to poachers. Around the turn of the century the Brittany moved away from pointing and setting and into dog shows in France and the USA, where they performed very well.

Dog Breed Characteristics

A. Protection Ability

Whilst the Brittany is a good watch dog, they do not have the aggressive instinct to be a guard dog. They are naturally friendly, and therefore not very intimidating!

Score: 5/10

B. Ease of Training

Brittanys are relatively receptive to training, but temperament does factor into this. Generally speaking, Brittanys are quite easy to train and respond best to firm (but not harsh) commands.

Score: 7/10

C. Playfulness

The Brittany is a curious, alert breed that loves to be active, especially when in the company of their owners. Temperament can be affected by socialisation, and so playfulness in this breed can vary from dog to dog.

Score: 7/10

D. Exercise needs

This breed has lots of energy and loves to run in open spaces. It's important that owners remember that Brittany puppies should exercise no more than 30 minutes each day, as this can put a strain on their young joints.

Score: 8/10

E. Adaptability

This energetic dog can sometimes be a handful, but not so much that novice owners should be warned off. Provided that prospective owners have a large house, a fenced garden, and lots of time to spend with their pet, the Brittany can make a fantastic first dog.

Score: 7/10

Dog Breed 36-40 Quiz

The solution to this quiz can be found in *Appendix H* at the end of this book.

1. Very intuitive and with an excellent memory, this dog breed responds well to gentle, positive reinforcement – they will quickly shut down and become timid when trained harshly.
   a) Brittany
   b) Finnish Spitz
   c) Great pyrenees
   d) Gordon Setter

2. This dog breed is very disciplined, and in addition to being an excellent hunter they also perform well as both a watch dog and a guard dog.
   a) Brittany
   b) Finnish Spitz
   c) Great pyrenees
   d) Gordon Setter

3. This dog breed is very receptive to dog training, but their high intelligence means that they will sometimes attempt to take advantage of their owners. Effective owners must be firm and establish themselves as the leader in order to get the most out of them.
   a) Brittany
   b) Gordon Setter
   c) Field Spaniel
   d) Finnish Spitz

4. This dog breed is a skilled hunter capable of taking down everything from squirrels to bears. As European clans travelled across the continent thousands of years ago, the purebred was crossed with breed after breed in an attempt to alter its skills to suit the geography of each new area.

a) Brittany
b) Gordon Setter
c) Field Spaniel
d) Finnish Spitz

5. This dog breed is strong willed and needs lots of exercise each day. They are not recommended for people who work long days or live in apartments, as the breed can be very demanding. Without sufficient daily exercise they will resort to digging, hunting, or barking.
   a) Gordon Setter
   b) Finnish Spitz
   c) Field Spaniel
   d) Brittany

6. This dog breed is eager to please, and its origin as a hunter and watchdog means that it is disciplined and receptive to training. They are very easy to train, and if given a chance they will stand out from the crowd in obedience tasks.
   a) Gordon Setter
   b) Finnish Spitz
   c) Field Spaniel
   d) Brittany

7. This dog breed was very sought after in nineteenth century France due to their impressive pointer and setter ability, and their willingness to follow orders made them the perfect assistant to poachers.
   a) Gordon Setter
   b) Finnish Spitz
   c) Field Spaniel
   d) Brittany

Dog Breed 41 - Lakeland Terrier

General Information

Dog Name: Lakeland Terrier (Nickname: Lakie).

Dog breed Group: Terrier dogs

Size Category: Small dog breeds

Height: Ranges from one foot, one inch to one foot, two inches (measured from the shoulder).

Weight: Ranges from 15 to 17 pounds.

Lifespan: Ranges 12 to 15 years.

Brief History

The exact origins of the Lakeland Terrier are unknown, but its appearance speaks volumes. It bears a strong resemblance to both the Bedlington and the Airdale terriers, but it may have been crossed with a number of additional breeds. As their name suggests, the Lakeland Terrier first came to notice in the Lake District, a picturesque area of northern England. These tenacious little dogs put bigger dogs to shame, as they did whatever it took to catch their prey – including tunnelling underground for days on end. Nowadays the Lakeland Terrier is a versatile and friendly dog who thrives as a family pet, guard dog and hunter.

Dog Breed Characteristics

A. Protection Ability

The Lakeland Terrier is small but mighty. They will bark loudly without hesitation and will show aggression when provoked. There's no doubt that this dog breed can offer their owners adequate protection.

Score: 7/10

B. Ease of Training

Lakies are independent to a fault, and can be difficult to train. Owners should approach this task with discipline, enthusiasm and a sense of humour!

Score: 5/10

C. Playfulness

Lakeland Terriers love their owners and will happily show them affection. They're feisty and independent, as natural born hunters they can easily be distracted by birds or other small animals.

Score: 8/10

D. Exercise needs

This breed should have at least one or two daily walks, each lasting at least twenty minutes. They are small enough to live in apartments, but will be happier in a home with a large garden in which they dig and run.

Score: 7/10

E. Adaptability

The Lakeland Terrier is not the most easy-going of breeds, but their quirky character compensates for this. They can live in a home of any size (provided they get enough daily exercise) and need quite a lot of interaction with their owner. With a bit of determination, novice owners will be able to handle this breed.

Score: 7/10

Dog Breed 42 - Lhasa Apso

General Information

Dog Name: Lhasa Apso (Nickname: Lhasa)

Dog breed Group: Companion dogs

Size Category: Small dog breeds

Height: Ranges from nine inches to eleven inches (measured from the shoulder).

Weight: Ranges from 12 to 15 pounds.

Lifespan: Ranges from 12 to 15 years.

Brief History

High in the mountains of Tibet, sheltered in the safety of Buddhist monasteries, the Lhasa Apso was born. Carefully bred to resemble a tiny lion, these adorable little dogs spent their days guarding the monasteries and keeping the monks company. Legend suggests that when deceased monks failed to reach Nirvana, they were reincarnated as Lhasa Apsos. The breed first left Tibet in the early twentieth century, when British explorers brought them back from their travels and today's Lhasa Apsos are faithful companions and dog show champions.

Dog Breed Characteristics

A. Protection Ability

The Lhasa Apso is suspicious of strangers, and takes their role as a sentinel very seriously. They will not show aggression unless provoked, and they are endlessly loyal to their owners.

Score: 7/10

B. Ease of Training

This breed needs a gentle hand, as they will become aggressive in response to a harsh training style. They are stubborn, but they will comply when food is on offer as a reward and they do particularly well in short, varied training sessions. Early attempts at dog training are difficult, but as leadership is established through repetition, the Lhasa Apso becomes more compliant.

Score: 5/10

C. Playfulness

In line with its noble origins, the Lhasa can be a diva. They can be moody but will also clown for attention, and will often make mischief. They are very affectionate and always ready to play.

Score: 9/10

D. Exercise needs

Lhasas don't need much daily exercise. Whilst they should ideally have at least one short walk each day, they will be perfectly content curling up in their owner's lap.

Score: 3/10

E. Adaptability

The Lhasa Apso can live in most types of home, and they are happy to be left alone occasionally.

This is a good breed for novice owners, but it should be noticed that their small size makes them vulnerable to cold weather.

Score: 8/10

Congratulations!

The sixth character of the password required to download the bonus book is letter l (that is "l" for laptop).

Dog Breed 43 - Lowchen

General Information

Dog Name: Lowchen

Dog breed Group: Companion dogs

Size Category: Small dog breeds

Height: Ranges from one foot, one inch to one foot, two inches (measured from the shoulder).

Weight: Ranges from 9 to 18 pounds.

Lifespan: Ranges from 13 to 15 years.

Brief History

The German word “Lowchen” literally translates to “lion dog”, and this description is apt. Whilst Lowchens certainly have a distinctive appearance, historians have argued for years about the exact origins of the breed – did it come from Germany, the Mediterranean, Russia or even Tibet? Nobody knows for sure. Lowchens have been at risk of extinction more than once, but evidently these little lions are as tough as their namesake. Whilst still a rarity, modern day Lowchens are still in existence and unlikely to go anywhere.

Dog Breed Characteristics

A. Protection Ability

Lowchens are deceptively loud, and will bark confidently in the face of suspicious activity. They truly are fearless, and will often challenge larger dogs.

Score: 7/10

B. Ease of Training

Reasonably intelligent, the Lowchen is quite easy to train. It's important that owners begin training this breed early, and, in particular, pay extra attention to reducing their excessive barking.

Score: 8/10

C. Playfulness

These dogs love their owners and will do anything for play time. They are very affectionate and full of energy – owners will never be lonely with a Lowchen!

Score: 9/10

D. Exercise needs

Lowchens should have twenty minutes of exercise each day. They enjoy long walks and make excellent walking companions, provided the terrain isn't too challenging.

Score: 5/10

E. Adaptability

The Lowchen can adapt to most homes and climates, but they cannot abide being alone. Novice owners can absolutely take on this breed, but they shouldn't expect to get much time to themselves.

Score: 8/10

Dog Breed 44 - Mastiff

General Information

Dog Name: Mastiff

Dog breed Group: Working dogs

Size Category: Large dog breeds

Height: Ranges from two feet, three inches to two feet, eight inches (measured from the shoulder).

Weight: Ranges from 130 to 220 pounds.

Lifespan: Ranges from six to ten years.

Brief History

The Mastiff is descended from the Molosser, an ancient guardog thought to have resided in Asia many centuries ago. These dogs share a formidable physique - Babylonian imagery has been uncovered of Mastiffs fighting lions, and throughout history they have earned recognition as war dogs. By the mid-nineteenth century the breed was in trouble; bull-baiting, bear-baiting and dog fighting had been outlawed, and without these brutal sports there wasn't much call for Mastiffs. The breed came back from the brink of extinction by competing in dog shows, and came to the USA during the colonial period.

Dog Breed Characteristics

A. Protection Ability

The Mastiff's history of guarding flocks and estates means that it is a brilliant guard dog. It will bark and show aggression to intruders, but usually its muscular appearance is intimidating enough to scare away any suspect people.

Score: 8/10

B. Ease of Training

Young Mastiffs are curious to a fault, and so crate training is essential. Obedience training is also a must – their sheer size means that an ill-mannered Mastiff quickly becomes unmanageable. Luckily, this breed is relatively easy to train (with a bit of determination).

Score: 6/10

C. Playfulness

This breed is quite playful, and very invested in the wellbeing of their owners. They are affectionate and attached, but will treat strangers coldly and with suspicion.

Score: 5/10

D. Exercise needs

The average Mastiff requires two 30 minutes walks each day, and will become destructive without adequate exercise. They have moderate energy levels, but can usually be found sleeping on their owners' laps.

Score: 8/10

E. Adaptability

Given their enormous size, Mastiffs need a large living space with a fenced yard. They are sensitive to disputes between their owners, and find it very difficult to cope with hot weather. This breed is a challenge, and definitely not recommended for novice owners.

Score: 5/10

Dog Breed 45 - Miniature Pinscher

General Information

Dog Name: Miniature Pinscher (Nickname: Min Pin)

Dog breed Group: Companion dogs

Size Category: Small dog breeds

Height: Ranges from ten inches to one foot (measured from the shoulder).

Weight: Ranges from eight to eleven pounds.

Lifespan: Ranges from 10 to 14 years.

Brief History

The Miniature Pinscher is a German dog which was originally bred several hundred years ago to kill rats and other small vermin in homes and factories. This breed is commonly mistaken for a miniature version of the Doberman, but despite their startling resemblance the Min Pin actually pre-dates the Doberman by quite some time. The breed's popularity skyrocketed after World War I when German and Scandinavian breeders increased their efforts to develop the Min Pin and the breed was brought to the USA.

Dog Breed Characteristics

A. Protection Ability

The Miniature Pinscher has a sharp hearing and a loud bark that they will use to warn their owners of suspicious happenings. They are regarded as exceptional watch dogs.

Score: 8/10

B. Ease of Training

Without dog training, the Min Pin will rule the household. This breed thinks that they are the leader of all they survey, and even experienced owners may need the help of a professional trainer to tame this breed.

Score: 4/10

C. Playfulness

The Min Pin is very loving and enjoys entertaining his owners by playing the clown. With boundless energy and a deep need for attention, this breed's playfulness can often be overwhelming.

Score: 9/10

D. Exercise needs

This breed has heaps of energy and is always in the mood for exercise. They enjoy long walks and energetic playtime.

Score: 8/10

E. Adaptability

Whilst they hate being alone, this breed is relatively easy to care for and will be happy living in a variety of settings. They are somewhat sensitive to the cold, but this can easily be dealt with by wrapping up warm.

Score: 7/10

Dog Breed 41-45 Quiz

The solution to this quiz can be found in *Appendix I* at the end of this book.

1. This dog breed is not the most easy going of breeds, but their quirky character compensates for this. They can live in a home of any size (provided they get enough daily exercise) and need quite a lot of interaction with their owner.
   a) Mastiff
   b) Lakeland Terrier
   c) Lowchen
   d) Lhasa Apso

2. Carefully bred to resemble a tiny lion, these adorable little dog breeds spent their early days guarding the Buddhist monasteries deep in the mountains of Tibet. Legend suggests that when deceased monks failed to reach Nirvana, they were reincarnated as:
   a) Mastiff
   b) Lakeland Terrier
   c) Lowchen
   d) Lhasa Apso

3. This dog breed can live in most types of home, and they are happy to be left alone occasionally. This is a good breed for novice owners, but it should be noticed that their small size makes them vulnerable to cold weather.
   a) Lowchen
   b) Lhasa Apso
   c) Mastiff
   d) Miniature Pinscher

4. Believed to have descended from the Molosser (an ancient guardog thought to have resided in Asia many centuries ago) and gifted with a formidable physique, this dog breed has earned a strong recognition as war dogs

a) Lowchen
b) Lhasa Apso
c) Mastiff
d) Miniature Pinscher

5. Given their enormous size, this dog breed needs a large living space with a fenced yard. They are sensitive to disputes between their owners, and find it very difficult to cope with hot weather. This breed is a challenge and definitely not recommended for novice owners.
   a) Mastiff
   b) Lhasa Apso
   c) Lowchen
   d) Miniature Pinscher

6. Without dog training, this dog breed will rule the household. They think that they are the leader of all they survey, and even experienced owners may need the help of a professional to tame this breed.
   a) Lowchen
   b) Lhasa Apso
   c) Mastiff
   d) Miniature Pinscher

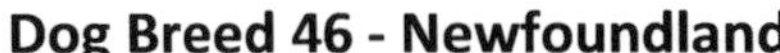

Dog Breed 46 - Newfoundland

General Information

Dog Name: Newfoundland (Nickname: Newfie)

Dog breed Group: Working dogs

Size Category: Large dog breeds

Height: Ranges from two feet, one inch to two feet, five inches (measured from the shoulder).

Weight: Ranges from 100 to 150 pounds

Lifespan: Ranges from 8 to 10 years

Brief History

A cross between the Tibetan Mastiff and the American Black Wolf, this enormous Canadian dog strikes fear into the hearts of all those who encounter it. In truth, the Newfoundland is a loveable and earnest companion, whose sweet nature was best demonstrated by the character of "Nana" in J.M. Barrie's Peter Pan. The future of the breed was flung into jeopardy in the 1780s, when the Canadian government placed harsh restrictions of the types of domestic dogs families were allowed to keep. It wasn't until the nineteenth century that the Newfie was saved when the Governor of Newfoundland declared the dogs his breed of choice.

Dog Breed Characteristics

A. Protection Ability

Given their immense strength and the ease with which they can knock down intruders, the Newfoundland makes a very good guard dog. Their gentle nature has led to them being named one of the best child-friendly guard dogs.

Score: 8/10

B. Ease of Training

Newfies are truly eager to please and respond very well to dog training. This breed is extremely large, meaning that training is absolutely essential (but it's rarely a challenge).

Score: 9/10

C. Playfulness

These gentle giants love to play with children, and have been likened to big teddy bears. They are very sweet-natured and love living inside the house where they can be around their owners.

Score: 8/10

D. Exercise needs

Despite their mellow nature, these large dogs need lots of exercise. They shouldn't be exercised too heavily before the age of two (due to the strain placed on their young joints), but once they reach adulthood Newfies can run, swim and play to their hearts' content!

Score: 8/10

E. Adaptability

Newfies are sensitive to hot weather and being left alone for long periods of time. They need lots of space in which to roam, but other than these three areas of need, they are quite easy dogs to own.

Score: 6/10

Dog Breed 47 - Norfolk Terrier

General Information

Dog Name: Norfolk Terrier

Dog breed Group: Terrier dogs

Size Category: Small dog breeds

Height: Ranges from nine inches to ten inches (measured at the shoulder).

Weight: Ranges from 11 to 12 pounds.

Lifespan: Ranges from 12 to 15 years.

Brief History

As their name suggests, the Norfolk Terrier was originally bred in Norfolk to kill vermin in barns. As their reputation grew so did their demand, and by the late nineteenth century Norfolk Terriers were being brought to Cambridge University, where students needed help with their rat problems. Over the next few years the breed fluctuated heavily as different breeders tried different cross-breeds, and this led to arguments about the breed standard, particularly concerning the ears. After World War II it was decided that prick-ear dogs would be Norwich

Terriers and drop-ear dogs would be Norfolk Terriers.

Dog Breed Characteristics

A. Protection Ability

The Norfolk Terrier has the capacity to be very loud when it wants to, but it's generally not recommended as either a watch dog or a guard dog.

Score: 3/10

B. Ease of Training

This tiny dog breed can be very stubborn, which can make training difficult. They are particularly resistant to house-training, and require a very patient owner.

Score: 4/10

C. Playfulness

Norfolk Terriers are always in the mood to play, either with their owners or with dog toys. They are also happy to snuggle up in their owner's lap each evening.

Score: 7/10

D. Exercise needs

This breed needs at least one short walk each day, or they will become destructive. They are also prone to overreacting, and so owners should make sure their pet doesn't overindulge and gets enough exercise.

Score: 5/10

E. Adaptability

The Norfolk Terrier is highly adaptable to a variety of settings. They are tolerant of most weather conditions and can be left alone during the day time.

Score: 8/10

Dog Breed 48 - Papillon

General Information

Dog Name: Papillon

Dog breed Group: Companion dogs

Size Category: Small dog breeds

Height: Ranges from eight inches to eleven inches (measured from the shoulder).

Weight: Ranges from four to nine pounds.

Lifespan: Ranges from 12 to 16 years

Brief History

The Papillon (whose name translates to "butterfly") can be seen in paintings dating as far back as the sixteenth century, and they were a favoured companion amongst European nobility (some going as far as carrying them in small baskets). The Papillon has a well-deserved air of status, and the breed was adored by Marie Antoinette. These tiny dogs arrived in England in 1901, where they remain as a beloved domestic companion.

Dog Breed Characteristics

A. Protection Ability

The Papillon is an excellent barker and excels as a watch dog. Their excessive yapping can verge on irritating though, and so extra care must be taken to train this predisposition away.

Score: 7/10

B. Ease of Training

This breed is highly intelligent and eager to please. They can pick up commands after just one dog training session, and they respond particularly well to food as a reward.

Score: 9/10

C. Playfulness

Papillons adore attention and will do anything to get it. They enjoy energetic playtime (particularly with children), but are intuitive enough to realize when it's time to settle down and have belly rubs.

Score: 8/10

D. Exercise needs

They may be tiny, but Papillons have lots of energy. They need daily walks, but can get their daily dose of exercise by running around the house and garden. They also enjoy games that test them mentally, as they are highly intelligent.

Score: 6/10

E. Adaptability

A good choice for the novice owner, the Papillon can live in small apartments or large houses, and are relatively easy-going. As long as they get as much attention as they feel they deserve, this breed will be happy!

Score: 8/10

Dog Breed 49 - Pekingese

General Information

Dog Name: Pekingese

Dog breed Group: Companion dogs

Size Category: Small dog breeds

Height: Ranges from six inches to nine inches (measured at the shoulder).

Weight: Ranges from 7 to 14 pounds.

Lifespan: Ranges from 12 to 15 years.

Brief History

Legend suggests that the Pekingese was created when a lion fell in love with a monkey, and begged Buddha to shrink him to match his lover's size. Whilst this may not be completely true, the Pekingese is indeed one of China's most ancient breeds and was a companion to members of the imperial family. The breed was rarely allowed to leave the palace, and so finding five unguarded Pekingese dogs was a treat for British troops during the Opium War of 1860. They were taken back to England as prizes of war, and many more dogs were smuggled out of China in the coming years.

Dog Breed Characteristics

A. Protection Ability

Whilst they are more used to being guarded than doing the guarding themselves, the Pekingese is loud enough to be an effective watch dog.

Score: 7/10

B. Ease of Training

This breed is intelligent and stubborn, which makes training them very difficult. Leadership should be established as early as possible, and owners will need lots of patience when training this breed.

Score: 4/10

C. Playfulness

The Pekingese has retained its air of nobility, and they expect their owners to cater to them. They are reasonably playful, but if they're no longer in the mood to play they will walk away.

Score: 5/10

D. Exercise needs

The Pekingese will proudly strut along the pavement when taken on walks, but they don't actually require much physical activity to stay fit. One short walk each day should suffice.

Score: 4/10

E. Adaptability

The Pekingese will take most things in its stride, but due to its small stature and fluffy coat, it can't abide hot weather. In most respects, this breed is quite easy to care for and a good choice for a novice owner.

Score: 8/10

Congratulations!

The sixth character of the password required to download the bonus book is letter m.

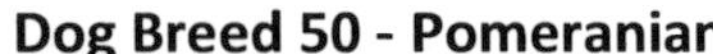

Dog Breed 50 - Pomeranian

General Information

Dog Name: Pomeranian (Nickname: Pom)

Dog breed Group: Companion dogs

Size Category: Small dog breeds

Height: Ranges from seven inches to one foot (measured at the shoulder).

Weight: Ranges from three to seven pounds.

Lifespan: Ranges from 12 to 16 years.

Brief History

The origins of the Pomeranian are a little mysterious, as the breed didn't come to be known until it arrived in England in the late nineteenth century. The breed was a favourite of Queen Victoria, whose little Pom, named “Turi”, was by her side when she passed away in 1901. Queen Victoria was not the only historical figure to become enamored with this dog breed; the Pomeranian was also beloved by Marie Antoinette, Amadeus Mozart and Emile Zola, and one lucky Pomeranian was even taken to safety on a lifeboat during the sinking of the Titanic. Today, the Pomeranian is one of the most popular breeds in both the UK and USA.

Dog Breed Characteristics

A. Protection Ability

Pomeranians bark a lot, but this is always intended as a warning to their owners. Their hearts are in the right place, but they can often be mistaken about exactly what constitutes a threat and what is simply a passerby or the postman.

Score: 4/10

B. Ease of Training

Poms are quite easy to train, and are particularly talented at picking up tricks. They can, however, take over if their owner doesn't establish themselves as the leader.

Score: 6/10

C. Playfulness

Whilst these dogs can be quite playful, they have a tendency to snap at small children and become resentful when they're not the center of attention. This breed isn't recommended for houses with young children.

Score: 5/10

D. Exercise needs

Poms don't require much exercise. Dog training sessions are a great way of giving them a little bit of physical and mental exercise without overexerting them.

Score: 4/10

E. Adaptability

The main concern with the Pomeranian is that they strongly dislike being left on their own, and they can be aggressive with young children. This dog breed is relatively simple to care for, but prospective owners should definitely take these factors into account.

Score: 6/10

Dog Breed 46-50 Quiz

The solution to this quiz can be found in *Appendix J* at the end of this book.

1. A loveable and earnest companion, this dog has a reputation as one of the best child-friendly guard dog
   a) Pomeranian
   b) Newfoundland
   c) Papillon
   d) Norfolk Terrier

2. This dog breed was originally bred in Norfolk to kill vermins in barns.
   a) Pomeranian
   b) Newfoundland
   c) Papillon
   d) Norfolk Terrier

3. This breed is highly intelligent and eager to please. They can pick up commands after just one dog training session, and they respond particularly well to food as a reward
   a) Pomeranian
   b) Newfoundland
   c) Papillon
   d) Norfolk Terrier

4. Legend suggests that this dog breed was created when a lion fell in love with a monkey, and begged Buddha to shrink him to match his lover's size!
   a) Pomeranian
   b) Norfolk Terrier
   c) Pekingese
   d) Papillon

5. This breed was beloved by Queen Victoria, Marie Antoinette, Amadeus Mozart and Emile Zola. Today it remains one of the most popular dog breeds in both the UK and USA. While they can be quite playful, they have a tendency to snap at children and become resentful when they're not the centre of attention
   a) Pomeranian
   b) Newfoundland
   c) Papillon
   d) Norfolk Terrier

Conclusion

Every dog breed is unique, and they each have complexities that cannot be fully appreciated at first glance. Big dogs may look imposing, but plenty of them are tremendously affectionate and caring (such as the Newfoundland). Small dogs may seem adorable, but a surprising number of them have origins as ferocious guard dogs (such as the Chinese Shar-Pei).

When choosing a new dog, prospective owners need to first consider what role they want their dog to play. Are they looking for a guard dog, a companion, a working dog? They should then think about the day-to-day realities of owning their dog of choice. Can they commit to the breed's training and exercise needs? Will the breed be happy in their particular living situation? Lastly, they should consider the breed's origins. Do they want a regal dog who thinks they rule the roost? Do they want a hard-working dog who needs constant stimulation?

Adding a dog to a family is a big decision, and should not be taken lightly. No matter what breed they eventually pick, owners should strive to give their dog the structure they need, the affection they deserve, and love them unconditionally.

Solution to Quiz

Below are the solutions to the various quiz presented in each chapter. Please, while we appreciate that some of the questions raised may have more than one solution, we ask you to choose the one you feel is most suitable based on the information you gained in this book (and not your prior knowledge). Enjoy!

Appendix A: Dog Breed 1-5 Quiz

Question	Answer
1	B
2	B
3	B
4	D
5	A
6	B
7	C
8	B
9	D

Appendix B: Dog Breed 6-10 Quiz

Question	Answer
1	B
2	D

3	D
4	B
5	C
6	C
7	D
8	B
9	D
10	A

Appendix C: Dog Breed 11-15 Quiz

Question	**Answer**
1	B
2	B
3	C
4	C
5	D
6	B
7	B
8	C

9	C
10	D

Appendix D: Dog Breed 16-20 Quiz

Question	**Answer**
1	B
2	A
3	D
4	A
5	B
6	D
7	A

Appendix E: Dog Breed 21-25 Quiz

Question	**Answer**
1	B
2	B
3	C
4	B

5	A
6	A
7	D

Appendix F: Dog Breed 26-30 Quiz

Question	**Answer**
1	C
2	B
3	B
4	D
5	B
6	A
7	A
8	C

Appendix G: Dog Breed 31-35 Quiz

Question	**Answer**
1	B
2	B

3	B
4	D
5	A
6	B
7	C
8	B
9	D

Appendix H: Dog Breed 36-40 Quiz

Question	**Answer**
1	C
2	D
3	B
4	D
5	B
6	C
7	D

Appendix I: Dog Breed 41-45 Quiz

Question	Answer
1	B
2	D
3	B
4	C
5	A
6	D

Appendix J: Dog Breed 46-50 Quiz

Question	Answer
1	B
2	D
3	C
4	C
5	A

Printed in Great Britain
by Amazon